TOPOGRAPHICS

Fragments of the European City

Stephen Barber

REAKTION BOOKS

Published by Reaktion Books Ltd
11 Rathbone Place, London w1p 1de, uk

First published 1995

Designed by Ron Costley
Photoset by Wilmaset Ltd, Birkenhead, Wirral,
Printed and bound in Great Britain
by The Alden Press, Oxford

British Library Cataloguing in Publication Data

Barber, Stephen
    Fragments of the European City. –
    (Topographics Series)
    I. Title   II. Series
    914.04

ISBN 0–948462–66–3

I received writing grants for this book from the Berlin DAAD (1993–94), from the Oppenheim-Downes Trust (1991–92), and from the Leverhulme Trust (1990–91).

I thank them, and everyone who helped me on my travels in Albania, the Czech Republic, the DDR, England, France, Germany, Hungary, Poland, Slovakia and Switzerland.

I specially thank Saba Komossa, Ingrid Raab, Aaron Williamson and Nancy Wood.

This book is dedicated to Kathleen.

1

The European city is a hallucination made flesh and concrete, criss-crossed by marks of negation: graffiti, bullet-
holes, neon. The city is an immense arena of eroded and
exploded signs – signs that mediate the city to the individual, and that individual to the city. For all their pockets of
stasis and stagnation, the European cities have taken on a
momentum of transformation in the final decade of the
twentieth century, and that transformation demands constant, obsessional exploration. The eyes of the cities' inhabitants are in a process of visual suffusion, compacting a
multiplicity of gestures and movements into the act of
seeing the city. The process of experiencing the European
city is one of corrosion, in which the screens of the city are
torn away, revealing layers and nodes of history and
memory that lie shattered by the trajectories of the twentieth
century. Just as it moves forward, blindly but sensationally,
the European city is moving backward in time, colliding
abrasively with extreme moments of conflict: the collections
of murder, annihilation, violence that make the twentieth
century vivid and tangible in all its horror. From this mesh of
space and time, which itself transmits the history and
experience of the European city, the imageries of television
and cinema are ejected into the city: television constantly,
droning with the noise of the city, and cinema intermittently, performing its dense projection of vision into the
eyes of its spectators. The inhabitant of the European city is
a participant entangled utterly in the visible, susceptible to
an infinity of aural and visual acts that encompass the
tortuous, the exquisite and a vast array of the banal: the
banal supports the city and gives it life. Assembling a city is
the most gratuitously *social* act imaginable, conglomerating

human lives into a mass of friction. To build a city is to subjugate the imagination to the obliterating power of the everyday. The cities trail limbs of suburbia that are the exposed and wounded sites of all the random residue generated by the glory of the European metropolis: racism, poverty, drug abuse, prostitution, desperation. The detritus abjected by the city and the strangeness exuded by the city are interacting elements of the same arrangement, of the same visual sensation. The city projects itself with a force which is exhausting, that in visual terms exacts surrender and acceptance of the city's appearance. The cities have a self: cities exist to be travelled in, worked in, passed through by the colossal ephemera of human lives. The cities represent themselves, accumulating a mass of vital imageries from the fluid matter of memory, nostalgia, evocation, and suturing that index of scars into the projection of the contemporary moment, the present and presence of the city in its immediacy and urgency. The survival of the figures that inhabit the European city hinges on a questioning of – a penetration of – the hallucination that is a city.

2

The cities of Europe metamorphose rapidly. Each component is dispensable and may be restructured at will at any moment: the arrangement of the city is constantly cut, impacted, expanded. The flux between the city and its inhabitants is a site of ferocious visual tension, with imageries generated that collapse and reformulate the perception of the city, its languages, its societies, its nationalities, its cultures. The cities have never possessed unity, and now the multiplicity of voices passing between the transforming city and the transforming individual creates an utter fragmentation. This aggravated sense of dissolution in upheaval is a source of anxiety, an upending of visual identity: but it also incites the exhilaration that is integral to a moment of reconstitution from zero, to a new way of working a sensation into the matter of the city. All voices must be interrogated in the European city – all media voices, sources, imageries and, yet again, 'the voice of the father'. After the Second World War, after the riots of the late 1960s, the voice of the father, with its power to unleash mass psychosis and mass uniformity, was rejected. In the radio voice of Hitler, the children of Germany and Austria had been made to recognize a father whose words were the very origin of their identity. That voice was corporeal in its penetration into the self. With the disgrace and death of that infallible father, every word transmitted by the media in the name of the father became a source of suspicion and refusal, always seeping back, always attempting to supplant. Every father that speaks, from Berlin to Belgrade, has a voice that the city's inhabitants must set aside in order to breathe. The refusal of the voice of the father is in the great tradition of the European cities, where the imposing image of the historical past is that of the historical void, and where memory is a set of blackouts, shocks and violences, interspersed with points of stasis. To refuse the voice of the father implies isolation, punishment, which the city answers severely in a visual arrangement of tenement blocks, suburban high-rise encampments, colonies on the edge of the city. However essential the act of refusal may be as an assertion of presence of the void of the city, it never prevents the reassertion of the voice of the father. The city resounds with a tinnitus of the aural media that is reinforced by every image that tracks and illuminates the inhabitants' daily round. The contemporary is endlessly at maximum volume and at maximum ocular speed and colour, unstoppable in its broken rhythms and cacophonies. The silence of the city can exist only when its inhabitant becomes stranded in the historical gaps of the city, where its past wounds intersect with the future, but where the present is empty, vacuumed of sound. In the last instance, no authentic father exists in the European cities, and the source of the voices is only the axis of a mass of divergent representations, that spurts imageries and languages in every direction. The European city compulsively invites its inhabitants to refuse the voice of their fathers; but however extreme or intricate that refusal may be, the city will always survive by inventing a new set of voices around another axis of sound and vision. The voices of the city and the voices of its figures are in a dialogue of the deaf, a dialogue in forked tongues – but together they produce the raw material that is the language of the city, into which its imageries can be assembled. The voices are at maximum potential after their extremity has brought down a conflagration, a choking of the vocal tract and the end of the city, as in 1945 Berlin: then the city is speechless and stricken, infinitely open to all languages.

3

A journey into the suburbs: the tramways grind through the arrangement of housing blocks where, from every balcony, eyes stare down. The longer the journey, the greater the sense of dilution – a diffusion of human experience into a blank tone of impermanent concrete, supermarkets, television screens. Even the graffiti that blast from the heart of the city has been submerged here, leaking away from declaration and obliteration into a description of affection and taunting: pyrotechnics over blood. The battles of territory, race, neo-fascism that marked every wall and tram-shelter of the eastern Berlin suburb of Marzahn have now been screened by new colours in the gang warfare of the lost city: a set of vivid but blank screens placed over the virulence and anguish which once pitted those walls like the constellations of shrapnel on the old grey tenement facades of the city. In these outer suburbs, these annexes of extremity, the sensation of an act of chance is overwhelming. Nothing could be more bizarre than the vast accumulation of human bodies and low-grade building materials on the edge of the city: a spontaneous concoction, born of intoxication and obsession on the part of its constructors. The light around these blocks is dense, almost tangible, punctuated only by the insignia of supermarkets, the incessant namings of shopping chains. If this European suburb were exchanged, by chance, with the blocks around a city in Albania, the operation would not leave a scar; the languages of the supermarkets could be reinvented with new numerals, designs, desires; and the tramways could ingest another population into the city. Around the concrete suburbs of Marseilles, the violent light compacts the lethal explosions of fury and indignation, so that banality is brilliant; in Marzahn, the light petrifies an already comatose situation, though anger exists in a parallel dosage, equally volatile and narcotic. The transplantation of anger from the city suburbs into the heart of the European city is a process of insinuation – the infiltration of languages and imageries moves in a great intersecting gesture from the metropolis to suburbia and back, so that European suburbia mirrors, frozenly, that which is intensely present within the European city, giving the city its burning core of banality.

4

At every step, something vital is missing in the European city. Trajectories from one location to another are interrupted by a process which is designed to clot the city into nodes of financial efficiency. But in the European city, such a bogus coagulation will not hold, and the city pours out its riotous haemophiliac pulse, irregularly but unstoppably. The trajectory taken through the city is guided by that city's voids, by what is *not* there. The city is constructed by its gaps. Now that the wars of the twentieth century have lost the carapace of their original authenticity, their existence persists and visualizes itself only in fragments – but fragments of intense power that impact raw past upon the present moment. Immense human gatherings upon the European city, such as the Soviet Army's final movement from Kostrzyn through to Berlin, are blank gestures in contemporary Europe, when set against the slightest thread of material damage or decay which is present in the fabric of the contemporary city: the evidence of loss is the crucial matter of the metropolis. The voids of the European city hold it together, haunting the city's inhabitants with a nostalgia for destruction that is also a lust for survival. New buildings must be discarded instinctually as inept apparitions, visual evidence of malicious will – since to build rearranges the complex network of the objects which *are not there*, and which sustain human balance by the permanence of their invisibility. Every European city has a twin that died at birth. The plan to obliterate the surviving ruined elements of Berlin in 1945, after the war, and to construct a new city some distance away, is the anchoring memory of the contemporary city: the void city with its void population is constantly resuscitated by the damaged fragments that carry its imagery and its memory. The entirety of

Europe now comprises an eminently missing city which will not conglomerate, which eludes its identity, which will not adhere to its own history. In the heart of its catastrophe, wrapped in the skin of its nostalgia for obliteration, Europe resides, in fragments.

5

The former Stasi (secret police) headquarters in Berlin-Lichtenberg has had its identity cracked and humiliated. Some of it is a supermarket, some of it commercial offices. The city was based around a network of gazes that had their axis in this building, and now that that axis has been crushed out of existence, the gazes swing wildly, in an undetermined helter-skelter of acts of looking. The contact between each human being in the city of East Berlin was determined by their proximity and by the terror which that proximity occasioned. Contact was based on the presence of omniscience, across scales and networks of tedium and banality. When the act of looking was made closely enough, it revealed a flaw; if that visual flaw could be welded to an oral declaration, then a representation of betrayal could be constructed. Every momentary movement of expulsion, abjection, refusal in the city had its source in the collection and assemblage, on a massive scale, of gazes. The carapace on the private life of the city's inhabitants became a surface to be flayed with gazes, and the more abrasive the gaze became, the less distance could be maintained between the inhabitant and the raw city. The arena of looking was built on such velocities of vision and sound that no compromise was too absurd to make – the entire configuration of looking and denunciation created its own bizarre identity, so brittle that it exploded in an instant. And one arena of vision has been replaced by another, in which the gaze has no object or source – nothing can be pinned down according to any system of recognition, or of guilt. The gaze is void, occupied bogusly by the imageries of the former Federal Republic; also occupied by television and advertising imageries, which possess alien multiplicity. The levels of differentiation in the act of looking, so complex and intricate in the time of the Stasi, like a pointillism of vision, are now attenuated. Eyes trained to see and skin the appearances of human behaviour in the city now have to move in every direction, simply to catch the textures of what is authentic, what reinforces, what endangers, in the detail of everyday life. So vision freewheels, 'Catherine-wheels' even, into visions of racism based on appropriated schemes of colour and of income – a spilling of the talent of such eyes, schooled as they are with advanced mechanisms of gazing. Every-thing, every inhabitant of the city, is seen at once, with a simultaneity which blurs into existence extreme amalgams of concrete, petroleum, air and flesh.

6

The extinguishing of memory is a tough, rapid process in the impermeable European city. At the end of 1993, I visit the Soviet Army's 'Museum of the Unconditional Surrender of Fascist Germany in the Great Patriotic War, 1941–45' in Berlin-Karlshorst. My visit evokes in me the sensation of an impregnable substance which, I feel, has disintegrated only by accident. The desolation is tangible, a sheer and unmotivated falling-away of power from an immense altitude. The Soviet Army's vast battle for Berlin left its layering of bones, fragments, ashes, bullet-holes in the body of the city, cemented by the volatile stuff of memory. The excavation and discarding of that layer is a gratuitous process, the utter *lack of weight* of which mirrors, oppositionally, the immensity of killing, of fear, of political and military domination. The eyes of the viewer see that the strata of memory bound into the city can only be disassembled in the most negligent, off-hand way. Memory has survived only through its own dissolving, through the intervention of exterior events whose tangential nature ingested memory, rather than assaulted it, in order to break it. The attention of the city moves off elsewhere. The city's consciousness of its own construction is oxygenated only by the present moment. Surface and interior exist independently in the European city, and its essential fractures are narcotically sealed by exhilaration and adrenalin – and by their visual and aural counterparts in the life of the city. The possessors of memory affect disdain in the face of memory's erosion. From his shelter outside the museum, the conscript guard blasts the avenues with his radio and stares curiously into space (while on the other side of the Oder river, the loudspeakers along the boulevards of the Polish town play

'I'll be your disco man' in an atmosphere of lassitude, lethargy so insanely intense that it must be a fabrication). In the halls of the museum, the absolute certainties and their unconditional representation sustain themselves with imageries and texts of death: the agonized corpses of the Nazis condemned at Nuremberg, each neatly labelled, named, photographed after execution. But the contemporary moment represents itself as an irrevocable shattering of memory, so that losses, voids and nostalgias become the transparent materials which attempt to seize the past, which the past sieves out and eludes. The mystery of memory is in its loss, the process of oblivion, which brings a flood of recriminations and a multitude of second memories: screens of memory, shows of memory. But the dirt, the ashes and the air of memory still lie around the city.

7

On television, endless discussions of the plight of Europe: a set of countries arranged in a sequence which backfires into a destabilized, crippled history. The vital question is that of reformulating the identity of Germany. Every night, the discussions and dialogues continue, faces and words flashing and ricocheting around a permanent internal paralysis whose representation must constantly be renewed, in order that it may scrape the mind into life, grate the latent violence into conflict. However much progress is made, in such discussions injected by television into the vocal organs of the city, there remains a barrier that is embedded in the very heart of the languages and imagery of Europe. This barrier, fluctuating in scale and impenetrability, comprises a central seizure of disaffection. In evoking the presence of contemporary European wars, a sense of exhausted powerlessness emerges (an absence of engagement with acts of domination). In evoking forces of racism, the sense of bitterness mediated is linked to the fear of renewed humiliations. So the subject matter must be presented rationally: one false word or image and the edifice will collapse into a psychotic hinterland of terrorism, extremism; into an unknown which, in Europe, is presciently and intimately known. Surrounding Europe is the instantaneity of the future, represented by its television, a kind of vast visual intake of breath before the aural rush which compulsively tears its own discourse apart. The great fear in Europe is the absence of that which channels the rational. The act of discussion is vital: it seals with language that disjuncture between the city and the wasteland, between the inhabitant and the homeless. Every night, the talking must be seen to go on, necessarily without presenting a solution or a formula, but simply as a vacuous act of language. It is extracted and abstracted from the sensorium, but represents itself visually as something inhabited by movement and dynamism. The discussion remains in progress, carried by the languages and vocabularies of conflict in Europe that carefully pare away the livid from the assimilable like peeling the skin off an apple. The European city must be swallowed whole by its inhabitants, and only the languages of television can force that operation through to its ingested end. The more voices that can be heard, the more soothing the rhythms of discussion become. The television channels of Europe multiply to present an aggregation of discourse. Moving from channel to channel reinforces the sonic textures of discourse, while the format of discussion remains monotonously stable, providing a visual basis for language. That language must possess the hypnotizing stasis upon which discussions about the identity of Europe depend.

8

Film imageries of demonstrations in Berlin: the city streets carry the human trajectories of upheaval across decades. In the 1950s, protests against the United States' occupation of the city: the film is bleached, and the demonstration is ceremonial, slow, surrounded. In the 1960s, unrest at its most ambitiously structured: the Vietnam war demonstrators appear in utter anger, set against the black night sky of the city. A burning, dense aura of revolt is thrown onto the film image itself. In the 1980s, mass gatherings against the United States' nuclear weapons deployed in Germany: again, the film is blanched, the skin of the demonstrators without blood, and chaotic sound impacts against the fluid movements of bodies celebrating refusal. In the 1990s, the black sky of the city appears again on film, with streams of flame across the decrepit facades of Friedrichshain tenements; few of the figures in these squatters' riots are visible, only illuminated constellations of debris, conflagration and screaming in the streets, ferocity in suffused lines that mark and configure acts of violence. The streets of the city were selectively imprinted by each of these eruptions (and many more: demonstrations against infamous names – Reagan, Honecker; demonstrations against the Gulf War). Plate glass windows of financial institutions shattered, walls inscribed with an immense catalogue of dates, times, places. The demonstrated city is an inscription in which assignations and destructions are compacted into obliterated time and space; an instant of conscious oblivion on a mass scale, leaving gaps in the glass screen of the city and adrenalized voids in the memory of its participants. In the chronological sequence of film imageries, the demonstrators are tracked down to their base, and expelled into diffusion; ultimately, they no longer carry the text which accompanied every counterculture through the streets of the European city, as a statement of determination, demand or declaration. The absence of the text is replaced by startling visual pyrotechnics, by a final uprooting of textual movement into visual cacophony. The European countercultures have leaked their text. The nature of oppositionality is enveloped by the contemporary visual media, which are themselves so vitally contradictory, so simultaneously implosive and explosive, that any friction, any unrest, is immediately contained and utilized within their imageries. Any message is made to work, as long as it visually astonishes.

9

Flying over the cities of Albania and Bosnia at night, over arrangements of light and substance, orange arteries across the suburbs, weals of neon in the centres of the cities: marks in the European land that gather density and structure only out of their distance from the eye. And again, it's by chance that one city is the site of desolation and another is the site of luxury, that one inhabitant is sated and another is agonized; to rearrange Europe would simply shake the pieces into an equally heterogeneous order. Instability has its axis and its balance, so that territories immersed in bloodshed and cities crazed by hunger will not pour over and acquire a pervasive existence in Europe: the segments of horror are rigorously, neatly bordered and controlled, from cores of petrifaction. But Europe also has the potential for a liquefaction of that arrangement, under the heat of heterogeneity that is generated by poverty, ambition, nationalism – and also by the most unexpected factor, the instinct and force of transformation itself that is always only a moment away from Europe, from the reinvention of Europe. In the darkness above the cities, it's no problem to imagine a land that is dispossessed or abandoned, leaving its tracks still burning away as evidence of the terminal ineffectiveness of the European city. Since, at rest, the city is a futile object. And, with the exception of the fabricated concrete cities designed explicitly for ephemerality, each European city is ground into the ruins and detritus of the former cities on that site, so that each living city carries the implication of its own flattening into shards of memory, and each living city erects itself on a great gaping mouth of irony. If Europe has an identity that is conscious, then the speed of its transformation must make it yearn for its cities to fall away and pass into the limbo of ecstatic nostalgia (the same nostalgia that possessed the nineteenth-century German architects who designed and built ruins for their cities). To explore the cities of Europe is to be immersed in the sensation of imminence, a sustained imminence of precipitation that the cities exude. And if a caprice of absolute futility were motivating the existence of Europe, it might invent a city that fitted exactly the entire mass of Europe, so that the lacunae of the space between the cities would become compressed and disappear, leaving a city whose utter resistance to the notion of the border, whose infinite disunity could constitute an image of survival for the peoples of Europe.

The Alexanderplatz in Berlin transmits leaden light from one concrete expanse to another – a numbing communication with more potential power than the television tower that pins down that hallucination of city space. The housing blocks around the central plain previously held up neon advertisements for the industry of Bitterfeld, a city where simply breathing in the air corroded the lining of the throat. Bitterfeld repulsed and ridiculed the human frailty of its inhabitants, breathing out poisonously with a magnificent brutality that negated every act of human existence as unspeakably inferior to chemical fact. Today, the Alexanderplatz carries less threatening inscriptions, but its terrain is still that of raw alienness made human home – its uninhabitability enhanced by its aura of dislocated resuscitation, as a zone of the city that continues to signal an intense touch of hell, imparted by the destruction by bombing of the last Alexanderplatz which occupied that space, under the sky and beside the river. In the European city, the subterranean strata which underpin the present moment have a fragility which incites expansion: the essential fracture of the city must be concealed in the process which envelops the eye in metropolitan vision, in the immense visual gesture of the city. But the scale of expansion also pulls the eye through the rough texture of the city, revealing its flaws along with the power of its rhythm, and the flaws point out the origin of the city as a cracked, improvised variant in a sequence of apparitions in that unique space. From the revolving platform at the summit of the television tower, the city's pulses and trajectories are laid bare for a surgery of vision. The networks of tenement blocks form a language of repeated hieroglyphs –

a language about the city that incessantly hits against itself in its attempts to formulate how such blank blocks containing people could constitute the city. But those collisions, constantly renewed in their incoherence and violence, are the way in which the city shows itself; while out to the east, the suburbs scythe radiantly away into space, since the city must both amass around itself to possess identity, and escape itself in order for its unbearable identity to be liberated.

European street gangs: the city, though a source of derision, generates blank space for inscription and territorial in-fighting. The street gangs conglomerate on the periphery of the city, as though its centre were alien, its identity posses-sing a vital component which the street gang cannot assim-ilate. The city centre abjects the street gang, and it walks there as though on barbed wire, blind, in a cell of white noise, expectorated. The street gang remains in the housing blocks, consuming the blankness which the suburbs feed out incessantly, comfortingly, dependably – since violence needs its structure and its nourishing support system. The street gang scrapes out the discarded debris of American music culture and maladroitly clothes itself with those ragged but virulent windfalls. Every year or two, a change of blood is needed, and the street gang disperses, goes inside to watch the sex channel on television or stands drinking at the outdoor alcohol stalls, cursing hopelessly. The reconstit-uted street gangs of Europe possess a homogeneity that is staggering. The suburban housing blocks are crammed to overspill, jettisoning their young into the dirt outside, surrounded by marshland and sewerage pipes, exposed to the uniquely drained light of the suburbs which over-illuminates every last detail of the inhabitants' lives. The suburbs pulse with congested blood at the neural interstice between the European cities and the outer space which is not a city; the street gangs embody that moment of traversal between chaos and the void, snatching at any appropriating identity or imagery that will constitute a presence in the streets. Now the tenement walls of Les Ailes in Marseilles and Marzahn in Berlin are suffused with that attempt at presence, with such repetition of lettering and colouring that the graffiti are utterly pure in their imagination of human existence; like the Bible, the graffiti are an enumeration of generations, so linear that each successive generation is instantly forgotten: they evanesce, and are transplanted upon, by the following generation. The street gangs use concrete for paper in a gnostic enterprise where the act of writing is so sacred as to envelop all human identity. The book of the European street gang is lined with sheets of whitewash, stinking of aerosol paint as other books breathe out their ink and carbon. All that is left for the street gangs of Europe is to enact and make books. The bogus neo-fascisms are so stylized that they cannot captivate for long even the most isolated inhabitants of the suburbs. All children of the European city desire an instant of life, desire some kind of explosion that will create its sign – a sign that may be as futile and banal as it is desperate, but a sign which will always be miraculously readable and immediate in the mass of the city.

Demolition: the transformation of the city is a restless process of negation. When the city is settled, an atmosphere of congelation rises to the surface, tempting acts of aggression against the city. The city is perpetually invested with a dynamic jarring and upheaval of its configuration. Demolition of the city's elements strengthens what remains, and also strengthens the sense of a vital damaging through which the city takes its respiration. Demolition by exterior forces exerts a particular force of poignant dislocation which remains vivid over decades (in the heart of Dresden, the black ruins of the blaze are still evident and displayed after fifty years); but it is the infliction of damage by the city upon the city which accentuates the vision of transformation. The visual arena of the city *must* move through concurrent acts of construction and obliteration, extrusion and intrusion, incorporation and expulsion. The periodic demolition of entire areas of the city makes its perspectives swing crazily, imparts a sense of exhilaration which is compounded from anticipation of a new 'coming into being', and from a lust for raw destruction. In the inhabitants of the European city, the localized vision of that city's upheaval generates the most direct emotional pulses: the transformation of the city is entangled with the transformation of the individual. The city and the human body determine one another through a dense network of imageries, languages and gestures – arrangements always based upon the power and potential of their own cancellation. The detail of the existence of each inhabitant is bound into the imageries which the city transmits, so that the slightest act of engagement with the visual languages of the city (choosing, rejecting directions while moving through the city; choosing, rejecting channels

of the city's television) forms part of that process of meshing, tensing, reconciling human existence against metropolitan existence. The European city's inhabitants are
absorbed by witnessing or participating in acts of self-
demolition – an involvement which receptivity to the city
inescapably entails. Harassing the self, screening the self,
provoking the self are necessary and natural elements of life
in the city. Confrontation with potential cancellation sus-
tains both the city and its inhabitants. Those inhabitants are
then adhered like insects into their perception of the city:
into their own cacophony of sound, into their own flux of
vision.

13

The Bauhaus in Dessau – the city still wrecked and shattered, patchworked together from pastel colours and the indelible marks of ferocious blasts of fire; a city at odds, with irregular tenements posed over wastelands as its heart. Abandoned villas, dirt-tracks and derelict neon signs lie around the Bauhaus, while the surrounding area transforms itself frenetically. Those changes compact and give endurance to the density and transparency of the building. The arrangement of the city falls as random debris around its unique component, the Bauhaus, the power of which generated outwards, expanded, multiplied and distorted itself across the cities of Europe: their housing blocks, government buildings, supermarkets, cinemas. The visual proliferation of concrete, glass and steel has passed over Europe, swallowing the light of Europe, infiltrating itself into the processes of transience and obliteration which Europe grinds into its own body. Every city in Europe is inhabited by the conjunction of material, time, space assembled in Dessau, then suppressed by the Nazis; the gesture of suppression and the gesture of infinite expansion together generate the visual tension that projects the cities of Europe to their inhabitants. To hold back the construction of Europe's imagery, as the Nazis did, is an act that unleashes a merciless reprisal in visual terms. The concrete blocks of Europe flood in scintillation, in constellation, across its cities – encrusting around the cities' edges and extruding through their skylines. But such a homogeneity in making and in imagining the city necessarily carries a bizarre process of decay with it, possessing such force and immediacy that the cities of Europe coalesce in their fragmentation, corrosion and collapse, from Sarandë in Albania to the suburban mazes of London and Paris. The building of Europe seeps as it repeats – and seeps time as well as money so that the sheer speed with which the concrete suburbs of the city are constructed is as breathtaking as their intentional shoddiness and uninhabitability. The cities are fired by an exhilarated impatience to build and see; by the desire for that constructed carapace to exist, visually perfect, for a moment, and then slowly disassemble itself, its progressive dereliction saturating and paralleling the dereliction of the human lives inhabiting it (until a new exhilaration is all that exists, the exhilaration of falling away from fixed space). Europe is such a multiplicity, since to see one building in its dignity and perfection is to be flooded by all the fractures of history and trajectories of vision that Europe brings down upon the eye.

14

Every text of the European city is misread; every noise of the city is misheard; every vision of Europe is mis-seen. The experience of the European city is one of captivation, but if you imagine that you are at the core and witnessing the 'essential', each slight slip in perspective undermines that captivation: you are at the periphery, glancing at a detail of the city, and nothing could be more inconsequential. The European city is an immense error of perception, since its pulses of stasis and transformation will shift at any instant, and whatever is built in the imageries and languages of the city will be simultaneously unbuilt. The city is an unendurable contradiction of itself and human life, with that contradiction given endurance; its nature is to contradict, endlessly. What remains is to mistake the city indefinitely. To explore the great elision of the European city – illuminated by its voids whilst given substance by its illusions. I travel to the eastern German city of Bitterfeld, two or three years after my last visit. I do not believe that the banal atrocity of excoriating pollution and depression could still inhabit the city, could be sustained. But on leaving the train, the same corrosive atmosphere is present. The city repeats itself; it negates its own impetus for transformation – it derides its onlooker with its blank stare of stasis. I walk to the chemical lands – a vast and complex territory, sprouting pipes, barrels and assemblages that have a hallucinatory intensity and intricacy – and through the deserted city streets which appear to preclude human existence as something negligibly slight (not functionally toxic, insufficiently industrial). But perhaps my mistake about the city's capacity to repeat itself suggests that I have other misapprehensions: maybe this city, with its 'palace of culture' and its ability to repulse and execrate unwanted visitors at their first breath of the city, is a paradise to inhabit, an ultimate fulfilment of human identity and aspiration. And maybe, if I returned again, the monochrome tenements would be transformed, the chemical fields levelled, gratuitously. The European city is an amalgam of astonishment and banality, of recurrence and uniqueness: its arena of imagery is an irradiation of false impressions, since what eludes unity transmits itself with the raw contradiction of multiplicity, which cannot be assimilated but can always reinvent itself; it is falsified back into unity by its witness, the inhabitant of the city, who counterfeits the contradiction of the city into the perception of the city. The European city is brilliantly opaque: it deludes, infuriates, eludes.

15

Travelling in Europe, year upon year, from Berlin to Budapest, from Prague to Tirana, from Marseilles to Geneva: the journeys accumulate into multiple screens of vision, compacted by memory; accumulate into a network of random trajectories. Sometimes the travelling becomes clogged for a time, in one of those godforsaken European cities where the trains stop twice or three times a day; but the remembering and the imagining grind on incessantly, since the European journey is a dynamic hypnosis which pulls away history from buildings, identity from the cities' inhabitants, imageries from texts. The journey has no linear velocity to it: even on the high-speed trains of Germany and France, the movement has a sensation of stasis embedded within it – lassitude compacted into exhilaration as the detail of the train carriage absorbs the eye, as the banks of graffiti cover the walls of the passing city suburbs, as the gaps between the cities expand in their homogeneity to paralyse the gesture of the journey. Europe is a site of dirt, steel, gasoline, flesh, and the relentlessness of the journey breaks down the coherence of each city. The cities flash and take on new focus, transformed from monumentality to detail, and back again; from a chaos of visual signals to the stable continuum of television or the cogent arrangement of advertising hoardings, and back again; from white noise to the pristine tone of a car exhaust or the perfect note of a slammed door, and back again. The imageries of the European cities oscillate between absorbed detail and inassimilable, swamping flux, according to the components of their volatile cocktail of vision. On the journey in Europe, the eye collects the signs of that flux: the names of alleyways and boulevards, the subtitles on films and the logos of television channels, the exclamations and price details of advertising boards. The journey itself has a language which has its necessary quotient of incoherence built into it, so that the act of travelling is at the interstice between viewing and being visually swallowed by the city. Assemblages of detail against scatterings of detail (vast vocabularies of detail around a single object, constantly transformed in the course of the journey) form the units of articulation which the eye takes, omits, blanks out. The language of the journey and the language of the viewing eye are tensely independent, utterly interdependent. The European cities move from being decorative arrangements to instruments of vital transmission in the act of viewing generated by the journey. And the European cities are at their most vivid at the instant when the journey is most suddenly cut and ended, when its obsession collapses in fragments of sheer loss in front of the eyes of the traveller.

Missing populations, missing individuals – the European cities lack whole populations that vanished in the World Wars (through deportation, conscription, massacre), and during the following decade of upheaval with the transplantation of populations from one city into the heart of another. The landscapes of the European cities are unevenly textured, apoplexically dense with housing blocks in one quarter, vapidly empty and pitted in other areas; the populations concurrently amass and respire, the streets dense with over-inscription and overuse in one district, under-determined and depopulated in other zones. The presence of the lost populations of Europe is marked into the cities as their counterface, the violent negation which enduringly aggravates the structure of the contemporary city, congesting or voiding it: and haunting it. The surviving European city is a conglomeration of renewed buildings and populations, grafted into the scorched gaps between the remaining buildings and populations. The deposed population cohered around the cause of its obliteration (around its political commitment, or its youth, or its assigned race); the new population is splintered, marginal, and with each new calamitous depopulation that the future of Europe will bring, the new population will fragment more and more: inhabiting the strata of dispossession which the city pushes seismographically from its history to its surface, and inhabited by the yearning and brutality which those strata exude. The cities mark the lack of their populations with monuments, the solemnity of which underlines their transience: the process of transformation in the European city is the ultimate caprice, corroding insistently whatever gathers most weight around itself. Or the populations are marked by a meticulously constructed and motivated silence, which attempts to conjure away the memory of the populations' removal as effectively as the human bodies were conjured out of visibility and out of existence. But each city exudes its selective depopulation through the fragmentation of the replacing population, whose imageries are the imageries of exile, and whose languages are the languages of loss. The missing population is sustained by those sensitive antennae of its presence in the city, which transmit it in rushes of adrenalized violence through the streets of the city, or in acts of narcotic or alcoholic self-disintegration; and in the cultures of anger and protest. The history of each individual in the city is one of competing integration and expulsion: the city envelops or abjects, and the traces of its expulsions delineate and saturate the future of the city.

17

The city streets at night: each European city is cancelled by the fall of night, its visual emanation dispersed and replaced by the tracks of illuminated facades, the glowing nodes of cars, trams, trains. The solidity of the city is transformed into the weightlessness of neon, emptied into shadows, pinned down by fluorescent graffiti spraypaint. The marks of the city at night form a text of repetition, in which road signals and station signs coagulate, restaurant names and nightclub logos deliquesce: only when the city at night is blurred and humming are its identity and intention lost sufficiently for its inhabitants to imprint their own identity and intention into its vacuumed framework. The night in the European city is a reprieve for the relentlessness of its inhabitants' perception, since night drains out the complexity from the city's arena of imageries and languages. The background of what is to be seen and read is blotted out, so that the inscriptions of the night are infinitely readable in their radiating monotony: the night is smeared and suffused with its imperative statements. To be read at night (as tracts of electricity, sodium, neon), those statements must capitulate to the transformed visual economy of the nocturnal city: every word and image must be hammered out to the eye with the absolute minimum of mediation. By day, the city is never immediate: its vocabularies are elided, inverted – they project themselves at tangents, in zigzags, in dense and entangled sequences. By night, those vocabularies are transferred to the city's television channels; but from the streets of the city at night, those languages appear only as chromatic flashes from windows, to be added unread to the volume of the city's light. The blurred tracks of the night city's articulation mirror the trajectories of aircraft in the sky above the city, the serial patterns of railway tracks across the space of the city: they exist to transmit the void gesture of their linear movement into vision. The European city at night is a blunt dialogue between what is illuminated and what is not. The material diaspora of the city's darkened elements (tenement courtyards, wastelands, forgotten intersections) is the night city's embodiment of the day city's population – a population that is subjugated, scattered across the vastness of the city at night, absorbed and ingested by that darkness.

I travel on the ancient S-Bahn train from Berlin, through the UFA film city of Babelsberg, to Potsdam for the award ceremony of the Fassbinder film prize. The prize is awarded to Derek Jarman, who is too ill to attend, agonizing towards his death in London in the spring of 1994. Fassbinder's own death in the summer of 1982 was a point of terminus for many of the vital film imageries of the European cities: an entire population of imageries squandered and lost in one accidental, individual death (Fassbinder caught napping with his cigarette still burning, his video machine still playing). The cruel and obtuse stubbornness of postwar German cinema disintegrated with the death of Fassbinder. And, worst of all, the contemporary transformations of the European city have slipped through the violent seizure of Fassbinder's vision, at the essential moment when their movement into manic overdrive would have benefited from the incisive, deadly wildness of Fassbinder's vision. The city unleashes its own imagery and its own internal friction; it pursues itself as a jarred and startled behemoth of imagery, insistently pounding, shattering and reformulating itself. But that imagery of the city must always be one of absence and frailty when it fails to collide with the creation of oppositional imageries, the work of hybrid filmmakers who inhabit both the existence of the city and the existence within which that city viciously envelops its inhabitants. The city's surface is receptive, sensitive, raw – it metamorphoses with each photograph or film frame that represents it. A central hostility exists between what the city is and what the representation of the city is. Each of the infinite number of tourist photographs of the European city interprets the visual aura of the city in tension with that city. In the creation of an imagery, the conjunction of the human figure and the city is always an unsteady arrangement. Representation intends to repeat and to contain, while the city is preoccupied by contrary, fluctuating processes of convulsion and expansion, occlusion and exhibition – and those are processes which preclude repetition. The city will not easily suffer assimilation to the image imposed upon it. The human figure in the city is also occupied by volatile processes of sensation and survival which themselves contradict the act of representation. Representation, the city, and the human figure: these are intractable and mutually tearing materials. The European city's receptivity to imageries of itself is double-edged: the city may absorb imageries multiply, inexhaustibly, permanently, but its capacity to dismiss, curtail and expel those imageries is equally assertive. As with the film imageries of the legendary UFA studios and their recreation of the city of Berlin, the image must actively permeate, flexibly saturate the city so that, finally, the image and the city will transform themselves together.

19

The inhabitant of the European city uses a set of gestures, an arrangement of muscles, a body of heat and anger, in order to move around the city. Trajectories through the city are incessantly interrupted, by traffic signals, displaced buildings, random events – and also by the barriers of imageries which need to be viewed, broken down into assimilable visual elements, before the trajectory can resume. The movement through the city is an alternating sequence of breathing: exhalation, suffocation, inspiration. And that rhythm of respiration takes on its own broken momentum with every city journey, so that suspension and dislocation become natural components of urban existence. Every now and then, trajectories through the city conglomerate visually, viewing an event (a traffic accident, a new information screen) which precipitates a momentary stasis in the city; but the hypnosis of watching soon breaks, since there is always an utter excess of visual foci in the city, and a steadily decreasing amount of time available for the eye to reach, strike and exhaust those foci. The figure in the city develops a particular configuration of bones, muscles, fingernails for its life in the city; that body of the city must be able to resist the parallel configuration of the city in terms of its jolts, its violences, its chaos. The city negates evolution; it subtly cultivates fragmentation in its inhabitants. The gesture of the human figure in the city is an intricate movement of locking the body into the city; the city is such a vast, abrasive mass, and the human figure so vulnerable in its inertia, that the figure must weld itself into the material and gesture of the city. Without the figure's original engagement to the city (to its languages, its imageries, its histories, as well as to its panoramas of movement), the city would obliterate it. The figure's capacity simultaneously to amass with the city and resist the city is hinged on dual acts of movement and vision. The figure appropriates the gestural rhythm of the city, but then jarringly terminates that rhythm when it becomes sustained, and metronomically *beats out* that rhythm when it becomes most erratic. The figure absorbs the visual and aural flood of the city, but disassembles the elements of that flood to articulate the unique metropolitan identity of the figure. The incorporation of the European city by its inhabitants is a bizarre process of traversal between the matter of the human figure and the matter of the raw city: the result is an endlessly oscillating hybrid, precariously breathing and gesturing through two worlds.

I walk through the Isle of Dogs in London in winter: it is a desert island. Where does the story of Europe begin? It has a thousand origins, in dirt and in glory. And if all the stories of Europe originate with the legend of Princess Europa, and her exile from the island of Crete, then they end, or are abandoned ignominiously, on the Isle of Dogs. The narrative of the European city is a regression staged on a transmutating site: the city is involuntarily pushed back into its history, magnetized by its own woundings and the need to cauterize them. The interplay between damage and reconstruction, between humiliation and affluence, is the most dynamically interchangeable and ironic force in the twentieth-century's treatment of European cities. In rapid montage, the majestically constructed cities become cities of dirt, without motive; the derelict cities become financially eminent. The cities most exposed to the stray impacts of chance are those most blind to the gratuitous reversibility which Europe conveys upon its cities, less as an act of history than as an act of sabotage: Europe is a surreal god of wrath. The Isle of Dogs is a digression from London: an annex which accords itself the status of an axis. I move into a house by the Thames on the night the IRA attempts to blow up the massive new skyscraper at Canary Wharf, and watch the light on top of the tower, flashing with extrumescent repetition as it illuminates the swathes of concrete across the night sky. The tower doesn't explode into erectoplasm (again, by the ghost of a chance), but over the months it leaks its human figures, blanches out its signs. Approaching the tower by day – on foot, in brilliant light – it appears incredibly beautiful in its dispensability: exactly as beautiful as if it were inverted and placed back down on its head, or as if it were duplicated endlessly across London, across the entire mass of Europe, with the same obsessive sense of purposelessness that animated the constructors of the reinforced concrete bunkers which are scattered across the fields of Albania, their empty machine-gun outlets facing out in every direction. The European city exists only to impress its own visual presence upon itself and upon the eye of its viewer. The cities' vast new monuments – the Grande Arche in Paris, Canary Wharf in London – sit with most ease and dignity when they have become emptied, and obsolete. Across the face of Europe, these monuments are interchangeable markings, random features. Only with their obsolescence do they become spontaneously integrated into the European city.

The transformation of the European city: while the eye of
the viewer is absent, the city metamorphoses jarringly. It
collects itself in new masses, expels itself into new wastelands; when the absent eye focuses on it again, the city has
suffered a jumpcut on a vast, metropolitan scale. The aim of
its transformation is to erode recognition, to create friction
against fixity; then that aim itself erodes. So the city is
incessantly unrecognizable: the stability of the city and the
gratification of its viewer are permanently postponed. The
pleasure generated by the city is found in the places and
sites where the city is not whole, where it has been cracked
by the force of its own irrepressible respiration. Viewing the
city intermittently is a process of unbearable and inexplicable anticipation, since any movement of the city in any
direction is potentially possible, just as any collapse may be
imminent. And the sensation of the city is, perceptually, an
instant away from realization. While the eye of the viewer is
absent, the city's imageries stop dead and its languages are
nullified: in the intervals between acts of seeing, the city
works with a static vocabulary of addition and subtraction –
its internal trajectories and arteries are blindly multiplied,
and its treasury of imagery is blithely subdivided. The
unwatched city suffers an epileptic spasm with sharp and
exact gestures, but confined to a temporal haze of indeter-
minable duration (a moment, a decade) where the image is
derelict – existent, but not transmitted, not apprehended by
the eye. But while the eye of the viewer is present, the city is
persistently exposed and enfolds itself. It explodes slowly,
minutely, in catastrophic panoramas of detail: the city
breaking through itself, every noise of disjuncture amplified
to extremity; the city discarding itself, every falling shard

projecting the momentum of its expulsion to the last instant. The city's space of imagery is assembled in a process of random pointillism, the vivid instantaneity of which is the inverse of the city's infinite proliferation: the real time of the viewed city is an amalgam of conflicting layers of image and text that impact into one another or pull away, alternately occupying and evacuating the space of the city. Enthralled in its visualization, in *being* visualized by the watching eye, the city shifts to the pulses of its own historical flaws, sustaining its transformation by *adhering* to the eye of its inhabitant, a captivation of the act of vision. But the eye of the viewer is always at a tangent to the city – the eye is swamped in the liquefaction of its own surface tension, gritted by the act of watching. The eye is the distance of a film away from the city.

The SS execution building in the suburb of Berlin-Plötzen-
see: the narratives of horror brought down to one line, the
hooked block of wood from which the opponents of the
regime were hanged. In the adjacent room, gangs of schoolchildren are milling around texts hung on the bare stone
walls – documents of the interrogations and accusations (the
executed made jokes about Hitler, expressed disquiet, made
passing remarks). Each narration sutures the chance statement into a detailed linear progression which terminates
with the date of execution: the arbitrary word murderously
homogenized. The schoolchildren disregard the monotony
of the texts, run screaming around the room: alongside this
building, the prison in which the executed were held now
houses a juvenile detention centre. While the documenta-
tion room is overloaded with information, the execution
room has no text. It is a statement of action. It projects the
act of murder itself, since to contextualize the repetition and
detail of murder would negate its force. In the yard outside,
earth from each of the Nazi concentration camps is contained in a memorial urn: the mixing of dirt abstracts the
particular circumstances of the concentration camp (the
source of the murdered, their numbers) in the declaration of
mixing and its irreparability: what is mixed cannot be
unmixed. The ashes are unseen; all that is witnessed is the
containment and the declaration. The dirt of genocide is at
the heart of human experience; but, simultaneously, it is
elementally banal, visually undistinguished. The statement
of mixture transforms dirt into memory by evoking collection, concentration. The projection of systematic, governmental murder by the Nazis, on the sites of murder, is a
sparse process which has few elements to use: texts, visual

traces. The text condenses itself, burdens itself; the visual evidence shows itself. The power of memory is in that density and its rawness. The sparsity of the explicit traces of memory is compounded by the vastly multiple city which envelops those traces – the city both embodies and overrules the uniqueness of its specific histories, by its own over-whelming processes of mixture, and by the velocity with which it transforms the visual and textual statements it makes of itself. Across the city, the intersecting traces of memory are scattered: the Bendlerblock military complex, where the 1944 assassination plot against Hitler was planned (the leading participants were summarily shot in the courtyard, others were hanged with piano wire on the Plötzensee gallows in executions that were filmed for Hitler to see); the Sachsenhausen concentration camp on the edge of the city, the traces eroding, burned by neo-fascists. The city does not emphasize its sensitive components; it holds them, but does not actively remember, does not differen-tiate in its overlayered, excruciated history. But the traces it carries are as irreparable as the act of incineration.

23

The surfaces of the European city are strewn with grandiose and ambitious attempts to imprint nationality into them, to transmutate the abstraction of nationality into visibility, into evidence. But the sheer tenuousness and intangibility of nationality in the European city is projected by the silent fragments of its over-emphasis, its over-materialization. The national city is constructed from the heaviest, densest materials (marble, lead) to pin down and prostrate the territory which is gathered into nationality, to give that territory a centre which magnetizes all trajectories in that territory. In the assembling of Europe during the nineteenth century, it was the power of the city which sealed the construction of the nation, closed the gaps in Europe and unified the diaspora of territories. The internal naming of the city – its squares and boulevards – collects that text of nation into its material evidence, so that the buildings of nation are suffused with detail and declaration; the central squares of the city amass into a cataract of congealed imagery of nation. The result is solid and static (the permanent representation of nation), but the vivid integral flux of the cities undermines and disintegrates that stasis – itself a stalled hallucination (the most intense hallucination being Hitler's projected national city of 'Germania'). The European city is a compulsive animal that digs a hole to hide its nationality, since the open confrontation of city and nation is a terminally abrasive and shattering process of opposed identity. The inhabitant of the European city is visually possessed by that city and endures a perpetual alternation of sensation. First, sensations flood the act of vision and the consciousness of the city: sensations of exhilaration, commitment, empathy. Then, those sensations are instantly emptied in the paroxysmal ebbing of imagery which the city enacts in order to transform itself; the inhabitant of the city becomes visually negated (sensation of antipathy, sensation of lassitude, sensation of nihilism), and consolidates the fractured nature of individual consciousness in the city by expanding 'identity' into 'nation'. Nation amalgamates the gesture for identity in the city (and for a space to exist beyond the city) with the gesture of active remembering, which itself unearths its historical stockpiles of humiliation, massacre, encroachment. That concoction is volatile in the arena of the cities of Europe, where the prefabricated concrete metropolises are soldered together only by the vocabularies and imageries of international television. The vital heterogeneity of Europe is itself held together by those television imageries, and by the collective memories of calamity that have been grated, instructively, into its inhabitants' eyes.

The European city at night is a bizarre blackout of its day-
time self. The city becomes exhausted by the relentlessness
with which, by day, it must circulate its imageries, in
profuse arterial movements and through multiple divergent
channels. At night, the city exempts itself from controlling
the proliferation of those imageries; the imageries of the city
are then free to lapse into extremity. The nightclubs of the
city's most frayed and abused districts carry an utter repetition of cacophony and light, generating the violent, sexual
reassembly of human identity in the suddenly unconscious
city. That city is accorded a new respiration: exhaling,
purring, blurting. A raw upheaval takes place in the sexual
identity of the city's inhabitants. The gap between human
sensation and the imageries of the city is stuck together,
momentarily, with the fluids of sex and dance. The city's
bogus advertising imageries of sex are cancelled; but what
replaces that imagery is just as structured and just as
repetitive. The excessive city at night, compacted from sex,
ecstasy and white heat, follows intimately the excess of the
overcharged media city of daylight. The city at night is an
intricately torn pulsation of light and sound, rage and lust.
The city's most perfect moment of extremity is when the
bizarre bleeds into the banal, at dawn. The acts of the night
are reclaimed by the details of the day: the unshaven skin on
the faces of streams of early morning commuters, the blaze
of orange and green against grey in the overalls of the
Parisian streetcleaners as they clean out the gutters of the
city. Each day, the city must reconstitute the sustained
chaos of its imagery – recreate its interposition and im-
position – after the fundamental disruption of the night. The
city is pieced together on its brittle, skeletal framework: it

has its systems and its screens, and its eyes that are ready to look (since the inhabitants of the dawn city are adrift, in the absence of guiding signals, and lock instantly into the rhythm of establishing the identity of the city by day). The city is a supple regulator of the flux of its imagery, and of the resuscitation of that imagery from the night's blackout. The morning comments discursively on the night in the weight of newspaper accounts that give the substance of text, an order and a sequence, to the ephemeral and apparitional events of the night. The city irrepressibly transmits its consciousness, and the cuts in that consciousness; its process is one of harsh illumination, grating momentum. It signals its losses of vision in the envelopment of its visual presence.

The European city is a deadlocked apparatus for living: its boulevards and avenues are so densely clogged with cars and container lorries that the atmosphere is a ferocious emanation of petroleum, benzine, diesel. In the chemically propelled cities of Europe, the breathing of the city assaults and excoriates, mindlessly rips the skin away to do its work of human contamination. The cities are jammed. The petroleum saturated atmosphere acts as a new medium for its inhabitants: a plasmatic creation for the inhabitants of the city, who hallucinate constantly within it, mentally inflamed by its rabid bite, intoxicated, rhythmically hallucinating to its toxic flux and movement (the gasoline atmosphere fluctuates in inverse proportion to the terminal stasis of the lines of vehicles which generate it). That flowing hallucination of exhilaration is infinitely necessary for the city's inhabitants, as the antidote to the implosive sensations produced by their catalepsy in the city (abrasive impatience, rage, nullification). The motoring inhabitants of the city exist in a corruscating medium of liquefaction; they can only escape in a mental side-stepping, projecting themselves into other zones of the city (like the suicide who cannot imagine the next day, the inhabitant of the city cannot imagine the next complete revolution of the car's wheels); but the everyday imagery of the city is a tightly drawn surface which resists and jettisons the incoming trajectories of the evading imagination, and expectorates them back into the stalled brain of the snared city dweller. In such an entrapment, the only visual recourse lies in enumeration, in which the Mercedes and the Trabant are exactly equal and interchangeable elements in the linear vocabulary of the jam, void vocables in the stuttered language of arterial congestion.

The inhabitants of the paralysed motor city cannot ultimately liberate themselves, but are the willingly absorbent recipients of all the imageries which can be layered onto the concrete surfaces of the overpasses, and transmitted from the immense constructions of neon light which tower over the buildings of the city's intersections, squares and peripheral boulevards. The more rapidly the images change, the greater is the sense of release for the mind in its gasoline pool, and the greater the affection generated for that embracing surrogate mother. (I was born in the English city which lovingly identified itself as 'the motorway city of the 1970s': Leeds.) But everything in the city fragments, movement reconstitutes itself, and at night the vectors of the city are lucid, the source of a new exhilaration of speed and vision which is gesturally, momentarily, transplanted over the tarmac channels of the city.

The detritus of the European city forms a layer between its history and its surface imagery. The city necessarily generates its detritus, since its processes of transformation and visualization have a contradictory momentum which reacts into abjection – which expulses and refuses – even as it creates. The city's inhabitants who fall (in poverty, in desperation) below its surface are in intimate contact with the discarded history of the city. The marginal groups of the city are saturated by the history of the city and by the city's intentional elision of its own history; they attempt to possess and project those elisions as clear evidence of injustice and massacre – the 1961 massacre of Algerians in Paris, and the dumping of the bodies in the Seine – and of a central deceit at the heart of the city. History is shredded from the present, from the selective consciousness of the present, with its imageries and languages. The act of making excised history resurge and speak again is executed only with the rawest materials: spraycan inscription into the dirt of the walls, where erosion and cancellation work assiduously. The inscriptions are re-effaced into the tenement dirt, moisture and shadow; the exclamation of one particular silenced history is repeated until another preoccupation arbitrarily supplants its predecessor. Occasionally, the conjunction of history and inscription jars powerfully against the surface of the city: on the blackened walls of Dresden in 1991, the graffiti draws parallels between the bombing of Iraq and the 1945 mass incineration of Dresden and its inhabitants; the unscreening of such histories is too deeply visible to be ignored and discarded. Detached from the present and its systems of projection, the marginal population of the city forever reassesses the detail of history in its dispossession and its relation to the detail of their own dispossession: the detail is inexhaustible, precipitating an absorption in metaphor (even street protests and violent demonstrations become tangential historical metaphors and commentaries, commemorations of detail). The European city transports its marginal elements through its history; the marginal human figures endure, adhering to the alien matter of the city in order to attack it, refute it and deny it. The city needs that denial so that, by contradiction, it may assert itself and its presence. The dereliction of the city contains a profuse set of traces, mixed into extreme juxtapositions of history which exert a visual captivation – sufficient for the starving inhabitants of the city to survive on, since it fires off a sustaining anger and indignation. The city will not engage with its dispossessed, but also will not obliterate them. It abjects them indifferently, and abjects their imageries. But it must allow itself to be inhabited by whatever force seeks to refute and negate it; only that grating contradiction can activate the ferocious life of the city.

27

The languages of the surfaces of the European city are interlocked with their effacements, commentaries and over-inscriptions. Whatever is inscribed upon the city is vulnerable to reaction, response. Words on the city imply an equilibrium of text with history, text with human inhabitation of the city – and such an equity cannot be negotiated in the volatile, visual arena of the city. One imprinting on the city's surface is constantly exchanged for another, which may expand or cancel the original inscription. Every new imagery of the city instantly becomes the origin of the city, momentarily, before its replacement. The original, definitive and authentic city is reversed into the obsolete city with stunning speed. Entire vocabularies of the city's structure may be wiped out, incidentally and summarily; the rhythmic naming of the DDR's cities after the founders of that state – Wilhelm Pieck, Otto Grotewohl – is arrested along with its infinitely repeated inscription of inspiration – Marx, Zetkin, Liebknecht, Luxemburg (Rosa Luxemburg, murdered and thrown into the city canal, resuscitated from that gratuitous brutality with a gratuitous proliferation of naming). In Berlin, the surface of human history is disassembled from the city streets; the language of the DDR melts down to a compact core at the spectacular Memorial to the Socialists in the tenement suburb of Lichtenberg, where the node of tombs (from Luxemburg to Walter Ulbricht, with, sadly, no space for Honecker) forms a self-reflected circle, broken from the city and isolated. At the axis of the tombs, a huge red stone block transmits the inscription 'the dead warn us' into a void; the space before it, designed for the amassing of a hundred thousand spectators to the historical emanation of death (and its miraculous reconstitution into the endlessly repeatable, inexhaustible text) is empty. The process of effacement is so deeply scouring that the remaining shards of an identity through naming become inversely illuminated (bizarre cult hallucinations of the leaders of the DDR, sources of a hypnotic affection which did not exist during their lives). Simultaneously with this collective un-naming (a linguistic socialism of obliteration), the graffiti on the surfaces of eastern Berlin become overwhelmingly saturated, gesturing and exclaiming an endlessly new set of unknown names. The street signs of the city are constantly overlayered, manipulated, distorted by spraycan amendments; the duality of the city's official naming and the random naming of its individual inhabitant is an inextricable entanglement, knotting into a still more ferocious virus of visual friction with each transformation of the hybrid text, and producing a blind and wild cross-fertilization of imageries. The city bears and studiously displays its vastly inscribed and vastly transmutating catalogue of graffiti, which is, at the same time, the sign of nothing at all and also the vastly intricate and cross-referenced *index* to the identity of the contemporary European city. What is marked in the city incites a cross-marking: a creation, a nullification.

28

The pigmentation of the city is a fine amalgam of projections and disintegrations: light and dust, flashes and splinters. The building blocks of the city form an infinite arrangement of colour gradations that intersect minutely with the textual content of the surfaces. Each surface is implicated in the accumulating opacity of the city's atmosphere; the inhabitant's trajectory through the city involves an utter submersion in that opaque medium, punctuated by moments when surface is broken down into seizings of history, language, imagery. The elements of the city's pigmentation are a pulverized and heterogeneous matter, dense with the debris of the city's history and its markings. The detail of the city is inassimilably vast, criss-crossed by internal processes of seismic relation and alteration which form the molecular layer of the city's visual surface, generating the aura of incandescent movement and momentum which possesses the city even at its most static. The surface of the European city is saturated with evidence and signals; while demanding to be seen, it returns the gaze of its inhabitants intently, multiply, so that the city glares. Its pigmentation is both vividly present, and also subject to discoloration from the excess of its own interacting components and their impact upon the watching eye. In reaction, the inhabitant of the city visualizes that city emptied of its detail – regularly illuminating and transmitting itself, and inhabitable. The inhabitant of the city imagines the city's displacement from the site where temporal contortions and upheavals have become embedded in the city during their passage through it – imagines the city exiled from its territory (as in Werner Heldt's paintings of the inland metropolis of Berlin transplanted to the ocean). The inhabitant's immersion in the city's visual mass is countered by the liberating reformulation and conscious deformation of the surface of the city by human perception (a psychosis of the city, an infection of the power of vision). The revised, imaginary city can only be magnified and sustained by its hallucinator for as long as its raw, real counterpart is unbearable. When the equilibrium is reversed, and the soothing dream of the new city is rooted too comfortingly, then that imagined city suffers instant destruction, melting into nothing against the stark and intractable detail of the earthbound city. The hallucination of the European city is returned to its zero point; the eye of the inhabitant is incorporated back into the reality of the city's time and vision.

29

The city's imageries collect and move along its principal arteries: the city is focused in the depth of its boulevards and avenues, enclosed within the great facades of its buildings and channelled in the rush of traffic. The signals of the avenues are a disparate summation of the city, opposed to one another and opposed to the city which transmits them (illuminated advertising boards and constructions attached to the buildings of the city attempt to unhinge their spectator's attention from the city, irradiate the spectator's perception with the revelation of the advertised product); but the city's avenues need the implantation of those signals, since they force the inhabitant to be constantly at unrest with the city, propelling the city visually and giving its matter movement. The city's principal avenues are necessarily congested zones of over-concentration, overspill, overpopulation; their momentum is menaced by stallings, disintegrations, paralysis – and it is for the conjunction of the imagery and the eye to regenerate momentum, swinging and panning between sites of visual signals. The European city is an oscillating chase between eye and image, conducted at breakneck speed and in magnetic fascination: the eye pursues the image, tracks it, stamps an act of vision into it indelibly, instantly; then the structure of the city's imagery shifts into a new configuration of attraction which pulls the eye into its elements. The greater the flux of imagery and ocular gesturality which the city can generate, the more its metropolitan prestige rises. The ultimate desire of the city's imagery is for an immediacy and instantaneity of transmission, so that the city, the imagery and the eye would be viscerally compacted; but the imagery of the city leaks time, tensions, absences, borders, and the interval between transmission and reception integrally contains a chasm of time. In the permanent exasperation of the dilution of immediacy through its *extension*, the city's imagery instead invests representation with texture, intricacy, multiplicity, so that the great avenues of the city hold an immense flux of trajectories, a vivid generation of visual life (in the absence or fissuration of visual immediacy, chaos is infinitely preferable to stasis in the imageries of the city). The tragedy of the city is when its principal avenues are re-routed and their imagery is drained. At night on the deserted Karl-Marx-Allee in Berlin (the huge blocks of flats constructed under the original name of the Stalinallee in the early 1950s, and designed for the Communist Party faithful), the buildings' monumental dereliction articulates the loss of power with extreme poignancy. In the avenue's homogeneous screen of dirt, its depopulated silence, its dispossessed majesty, there exists the fall of the European city: nothing is more rending for the city than the cancellation and reversal of its imagery.

30

I travel to the Sachsenhausen concentration camp with the French writer Pierre Guyotat, whose family were active in the French Resistance. A number of them were deported to the concentration camps – an aunt who survived Ravens-brück, an uncle who was killed at the age of twenty-three in Sachsenhausen. I have visited the camp before, and found it bizarrely unevocative (beside, say, Dachau, which is agoniz-ing, exhausting): the camp was maintained as a site of internment and mass killing by the occupying Soviet forces until 1950, and in 1991 the film shown in the camp cinema was a blunt, furious declaration of atrocity, dubbed into German from its Russian source, using footage taken soon after the camp's change of ownership (a change tangible only in the sense that the inmates were then starved to death, rather than shot, poisoned and hanged as they had been under the camp's original regime). No explicit attempt is made by the present maintainers of the camp to put forward the fact of genocide, and so it seeps through the skin of the place with a raw but banal acidity. The presence of killing clings haphazardly to the site, in tenuous frag-ments all the more visceral for their arbitrariness. The site insidiously represents itself to the eye. Sachsenhausen gathers controversy because of its close proximity to Berlin (there have been many scandals about the future of the site, the plan to construct a supermarket at its edge, the arson attack staged by neo-fascists); the suburban town of Ora-nienburg only grinds to a halt at the gates to the camp. We walk over the wasteland between the few remaining bar-racks, the ruins of the crematorium oven, the site of the gallows; the ground is so void and open that the sky presses down, expanse upon expanse, crushing. On the walls of the barracks are pinned photographs and messages from people still trying to trace family members lost in the years of opaque upheaval after the war; they contend with the immense emanation of oblivion (absence of imagery, scraps of irrecuperable and eroded text) which the camp exudes. And the compulsion to make the traces and details of the camp tangible is countered by its oppressively undetermined and abstract atmosphere of dereliction. We can never *seize* the ashes, the traces of terror, the numbers of the murdered (with their subdivisions into the categories of the resistants, of the persecuted). The presence of massacre in such a site of effusive oblivion is infinitely detached from the multiple, complex imageries we know by heart of the concentration camps, in fiction and in documentary, in film and in television. In the building housing the medical rooms, the detail of torture is cinematically jarring, but mimics the horror film, rather than the documentary: a lampshade made of stretched human skin, a skull used as a paperweight. Pierre breaks a piece of tile from the wall of the cellar, used to store corpses before incineration; he will break it into living fragments of memory for his family.

31

The texts of the city form great libraries of interrogation, exploration, advocation. The reading of the European city requires a multi-dimensional ocular manoeuvre which is relentlessly repeated and renewed: linear, inverted, vertical, horizontal. The pivoting eye collects a mass of text during the daily round in the city: texts that adjunct into conscious-ness ephemerally and then disperse without trace; texts that survive in consciousness either by justifying their necessity or by pinioning themselves inextricably into vision, into consciousness. The refuse of text lies scattered around the city streets, from the contents listings of empty packets to the redundant narratives of newspaper type; the archives of the city's television stations contain the immense over-lapping texts of discussion programmes, news bulletins and commentaries. In the limbo of the archive, their textual speed and respiration remain the same, while their temporal framework has become irreparably detached, compacted and collapsed into history and non-history. The text of the city is inexhaustible since it is fed by the immense mass of the city's visual sources and inscriptions – even if every eye in the city were used to read the contents of the graffiti tags written over the plastic seating of the city's underground trains, their inventory of repetition could not be enveloped and catalogued. The text exceeds the eye, through its unique gesture and through its banal recurrence. But the city itself exceeds the text, since it possesses an endless desert of surfaces. And those surfaces, to be imminently present as the contemporary city, must perpetually expel or transform its text, which becomes instantly, obsolescently *hooked* into the history of text, the etymography of text, the design and dynamics of text. The act of reading the city cancels the vital and irrational power of the text, which becomes located and transacted. To be unassailably and enduringly identical to itself, the text of the city would need to be sealed over with a resistant, unreadable carapace. (The greatest text of the contemporary city: Anselm Kiefer's monumental library of lead books, constructed in lead so as to survive the impact of a nuclear holocaust, and his accompanying paintings of the gates to the European cities of the dead, painted in ashes to survive the onset of a human holocaust.) The inhabitants of the city are absorbed in an oppositional rapport with the text of their city, which, if unscreened, will interpolate itself into the identity of the city's inhabitants and expand obsessively, to occupy and direct the consciousness and vision of the city. But the inhabitants of the city also possess the potential to disrupt and recreate the matter of the city's text, excise its components at will, visualize it in its rawness, and read it as a directed text of the human figure's identity in the city.

32

The European city excavates its trajectories through the faces of its inhabitants, so that the faces incorporate the city as a surface of lines, textures, marks, scars. The dirt of the city rapidly builds upon the surface skin of the city's inhabitants, and any face caught in stasis in the street will be encrusted with the expulsive languages of the city as pervasively as is the surface of the city's buildings. Facing one another, on subway trains or across the counters of the supermarkets, the inhabitants of the city read the world of the city in negative, exposed and printed, in each other's faces. The detail is minute but disproportionate: a catastrophe in the city may be traced by the slightest flaw upon the surface of the human face, while a chance occurrence of no duration in the city may have left an inversely corresponding laceration: accumulating layers of each individual history of the face and the city. All that the face exudes is the collision of itself with the city. The faces of the city are incoherent configurations, rocked by the screaming, blinding present moment of the city. The faces recognize themselves and one another only by the arrangement of that incoherence, which collects around the eyes – the face's most sensitive and receptive terrain for the marks of abrasion exerted by the city. Lines are intricately gestured around the eyes as vectors emerging from the site of vision. In the photography and in the cinema of the individual in the city (that of John Deakin, of Leos Carax), the stare of the face is assembled out of its encounters with the city. It propels that intersection into visibility. The incisions generated by encounters in the city form a subtle scarification of the face, the surface of which is indelibly eroded and indented in parallel with the terrain of the city. The incisions are multiplied profusely, into every shifting population of faces in every street of the city, to constitute the great scar of the city's identity. In close-up, the image of the face moves outside the time of the city; in its separation from the city, the face reveals captivation, astonishment (the city is an enchantment of vision whose pure exhilaration expels an acidic detritus which chaotically gathers in the face). In autonomy, the face would be subject only to uniform processes of ageing; but the faces of the city are bizarrely heterogeneous, since the city contradicts the rhythms of erosion which are integral to the face – supplants, accelerates, distorts them. The face projects the ongoing contradiction of its matter with the incoming upheaval of the city.

33

With its masses of video cameras and observation screens, the European city is relentlessly supervised and surveyed by a power that is cancelled from its moment of conception. The visual fact of surveillance is one negated from its institution. No city can be ordered, however determined or obsessive the intention to exert that order in the city may be. The attempted structuring of the city into carefully controlled zones of silence, calm and inertia would presuppose that the inhabitants of the city are willing passively to accept the visual dynamics of a city; instead, they compulsively disorder it, set it into flux and chaos, and selectively obliterate it. An ordering of the city would need to control all of its clashing languages and images, together with every dimension of their interrelation. So, any rebellious malfunction in the elements of the city (or, even, any malfunctioning *detail* of any element) would precipitate a total shutdown of order. Every European city has its 'organisms of supervision': police forces, traffic controllers, department store detectives. The role of permanently watching the city and channelling the city's population (the inhabitant of the city enters and is expelled from the city through a valved network of prohibitions and recognitions) is multiplied and amalgamated into groups, since to view collectively in itself creates a great source of power. The more that any element of the city is focused upon, in a coagulation of visual trajectories, the more that element will define itself and become detached from the city's integral impulse towards erosion: flux is hallucinated into order by the professional spectators of the city's surfaces and screens. The supervision of the city is a delicate procedure of apparition, poised between amassments of presence (sudden saturations of

police on the streets and underground trains) and sus-
pensions of presence (the supervision of the city is suffer-
able only in its withdrawal and absence). A void layer
subsists between the city and its order, and between the city
and the systems of co-ordinated viewing imposed upon it.
The inhabitants of the European city streets are incessantly
supervised in a jarring montage of video images – an
accumulation of traversals of the figure across the focus of
cameras which inexhaustibly record the spaces outside
banks, railway stations, institutions, for the instance and
implication of their momentary human occupation. The
determination to record and supervise proliferates
outrageously and unsustainably (the DDR's Stasi police
used *millions* of inhabitants to supervise millions of others to
the minutest, most obsessive detail). But the arbitrary intent
of supervision is shadowed by its negation in the visually
resistant city. The city possesses sites which refuse surveillance, where the identity of human existence is hinged on its
ferocious autonomy and distance from exterior observation.
When the act of viewing acquires too forceful a momentum
towards a unity of vision, it serrates those sites of the city,
which detonate into violence. The eye of supervision is
utterly exposed to its own senseless blindness, and finally,
to its potential *blinding* by the subject of its oppressive focus.

34

The European city infiltrates disquiet into its inhabitants: the sensation of unease is generated by the damage the inhabitants may exert upon the city and, in reaction, the potential upheaval within which the city may enmesh its inhabitants. Anticipation in the city rides a sheer edge between exhilaration and unease: the conflict of inhabitation is imminently resoluble (in any of the infinitely hybrid configurations of human identity absorbed in the city), imminently inflammable. It is prolonged in an intricate confrontation of point-blank proximity – the imagery of the human figure and the imagery of the city are attracted and locked in cohabitation. The transformation of Europe since 1989 has led to a new system of underpinning for its cities: the expectation of transformation (and its converse movement, the lapse of transformation) constitutes a regularization of unease for the inhabitants of the European cities. The momentum of transformation is soothing, however much it may make the matter of history gape; the imageries of transformation flare vividly and adhere to the eye (the eye without object would be unbearably open). The scorching intensity of the process ensures that later, in retrospect, the transformation can only be viewed within an immersing gel of banality. The illegible detail of the European city grinds on, whatever transformation takes place. The inhabitants of the city fix themselves into the benign medium of detail, and screen themselves from the panoramic emanation of the panicked city. In the enclosed world of detail, a collapse may come only once in many decades, but then it will be overwhelming. Out in the exterior of the city, the inhabitants experience transformation as a visual gesture of transplantation. Even the inhabitants of the most displaced cities – cities whose habitual imageries have fallen away utterly, to be replaced with an imagery alien to every human sense – can rapidly assimilate their experience of transformation into the experience of metropolitan identity. The skin of the alien is embraced and rapidly dissolved. It then forms part of the surface of the city, and is incorporated into the city. But however abruptly they may be discarded, the ejected original imageries of the city remain indestructible; in their disappearance from the face of the city, they exist virtually – these imageries are exiles, radiating a sensation of mutated nostalgia to their former spectators. The process of transformation in Europe does not in itself aggravate the unease which is an essential element of respiration in its cities; but the detritus which transformation brings along with it is a presence that declares murder, robbery, insanity – it holds the eternally threatened shock of suddenness, of obliteration, which alarms and convulses the inhabitants of the European cities.

35

The European city, when released into the act of consumption, will consume itself interminably: consume its imageries, its languages, its productions, its creations. The speed of consumption is geared to that at which imageries can be generated onto the surfaces and screens of the city, but the speed of consumption must always exceed, by the slightest margin, the rate of visual production, so that an edge of momentum carries consumption on in raw and undirected sequences of ingestion and expulsion. The consumption of the city is welded with processes of the image's survival: the image reconstitutes itself vitally from its own disappearance, exhaustion or obliteration, and that process repeats itself multiply and relentlessly across the arena of the city, so that the city transmits itself. Occasionally the city will become clogged by the intersecting momentums of its spheres of consumption and lapse into an amassed petrescence which, even in stasis, remains evocatively articulate and bluntly expressive (in the sense in which the cinema director Douglas Sirk would claim that in his films, Rock Hudson *embodied* petrifaction). Prague, in the first years of the 1990s, was consumed by that stultifying, heterogeneous force of invasive consumption which stunned the memory of the city like an electroshock to the head, but left intact its exquisite radiation of lust meshed with etiquette. The population of the city is infinitely attached to the consumption of the city, and attuned to the rhythm of vicissitude that consumption exerts on the city. Each act of consumption also imposes an absence upon the consumer: a lessening of the potential enumeration of consumption, which corresponds to a lessening in the visual and acquisitional means of the city's inhabitants. The alternation of consumption is a source of pleasure: the tension between the void and its repletion, mediated by sensitive acts of vision – surveying, exploring, probing. But consumption also has its no-go areas: zones where the marginal inhabitants' visual tracking may only move from one void to another void. The inhabitant abjected from the act of consumption is still saturated, still permeated by its imagery, since even the inhabitant most removed from the interacting worlds of consumption – by temperament, commitment, resistance, poverty – is intimately exposed to those worlds; they envelop the inhabitant's space of exile and make that space transparent to consumption, visually magnetized to consumption. Consumption has a language and imagery which are hauntingly appropriative of human identity, which give consumption access to consciousness and to the gaps between consciousness (so that its vocabularies are exactly repeated while the mind swims). But consumption is gratingly opposed to the processes of disintegration which act upon the city – erosion is not recuperable, will not be reconstituted – and the city veers and detours, wildly and unstably, into its own material, while consumption must rest directly on its visual surface to exist in its projection. To sustain itself, to be seen and imagined, consumption must discipline the city.

36

I watch Wim Wenders' film about the city of Berlin, *The Wings of Desire*: years after its release, the film is overtaken by the city whose imagery it recreated and transformed. The film's viewing necessarily oscillates between its own two layers of time (Berlin in the late 1980s, and – fragmentarily – Berlin in its wartime destruction) and the flux of the present in Berlin, around which the film's time pivots with alternate prescience and gaucheness. Many of the film's most vivid images are now drained; conversely, images which were arcane or incidental at the moment of the film's release are now astonishingly apparent: Otto Sander's angel, in the car being driven from Gleisdreieck to the film set in 1980s Berlin, looking from the window at the devastated streets of wartime Berlin (now the streets are devastated once more, in a rash of demolition and reconstruction). The momentary images of the East Berlin streets, deserted and lined homogeneously with Trabant cars, are suffused with the imminence of the transmutation of those streets. The film's detail of agony – traced through random trajectories of vision, building to building and street to street – possesses a resolution which now foregrounds itself intensely: the swarming gestures of birds above the city, the embracing figures in the streets. The film is traced over a city space whose contour and predominant detail have been lost, and in that upheaval, the incidental detail gathers emotion around itself profusely, to endure as an image. The film is an exploration of narrative subjected to the city, in its endless process of splits, multiplications, openings, abandonments. The library, the Staatsbibliothek, is projected in its aural proliferation as a ferocious, multilingual babel whose collective momentum separates out into shards of interrogation and narration, upon which the sustained incoherence of the city's noise repeatedly falls. The aural envelopment in the narrative of the city is collided with the visual initiation of narrative – the opening of books, the inscription of the first words. Curt Bois' aged 'teller of stories' is a figure exhausted by the perpetual elision of narrative, but who persistently attempts to locate the non-existent site of the origin of narration. In the final scenes in the Esplanade ballroom (before leaking into the future), the film cancels the multiplicity of its narration, to assemble its pre-eminent image, reinforced and justified textually, as one of human resolution (man and woman as the embodiment and realization of the city and its entire population). The image is attenuated by the city which the film has created, as a chance space of uncollected visual trajectories, of layers of texts propulsively moving away from one another. An imagery of the inhabited city on film is openly irresolvable: the city's impact and the human figure's impact are visual counter-movements.

37

The Wings of Desire leaks into *Faraway, So Close!*: now Berlin is an uncontainable sprawl, provisionally malignant, and invaded rather than liberated. The circulation and evanescence of the angels' trajectories through the city is arrested: the evocation of internal human weight, the propulsion of blood through the body, emphasizes a potentially implosive catastrophe of the figure in the city. The voices of the city are now subdued, collapsed by transformation, no longer accumulating in a multiple cacophony of inassimilable origin: the voices are splinters and blurs, complaints and commentaries. Natassja Kinski's angel projects the effusive melancholy of too rapid a transmutation in the matter of the city, outmanoeuvring its inhabitants, who lapse into a misery of lassitude. Since movement has been constrained by the impact of a too sudden opening of visual filters, memory too becomes stultified: the inhabitants cannot recognize and collect memory from the surfaces of the city. The film takes place in an interstice of memory: all it recalls is the duration since the moment of the last film, six years before (the daughter of the trapeze artist Marion and the fallen angel Damiel embodies that sense of a human resilience and duration pitched against the fragmentation of memory); the film is pitted and framed with building-sites and wastelands which visualize the void of memory. The velocity of the eye travelling high over and into the city of *The Wings of Desire* is brought down to earth and dirt. The city of *Faraway, So Close!* is one which endangers and isolates its inhabitants. While the first film pivoted on the desired cocooning and magnetization of its inhabitants, in the second the internal flux of the city into its inhabitants' consciousness becomes volatile, noxious. The interrogation of narration as a means of narrative in *The Wings of Desire* is abandoned in the second film: the exploration of narration is ripped away along with memory (what little subsists of narrative is as chaotic and crass as the surface of the city it projects). The death and resuscitation of Otto Sander's angel at the close of the film is not the resuscitation of the city, which is left in silence and abandonment: when a trajectory is finally established, it is external – the river barge journey north, moving away from Berlin – and utterly random (when the lovers of Carax's *Les Amants du Pont Neuf* abandon Paris, it is an act of exhilarated self-expulsion, and directed towards the ocean; and when Herzog's *Fitzcarraldo* leaves the Brazilian city, it is to execute obsession). The city of *Faraway, So Close!* is disordered and stunned by its visual upheaval, and exacts loss from its inhabitants: it creates a diaspora of narration and memory, a diaspora of sensation.

38

The desire for a film imagery of the European city is compulsive but unrealizable. The city inhabitants are caught in the visual contradiction of the city, which narcotically spikes and unravels their lives. The violent gesture of the city's presence is intricate, split between transformation enacted upon the city's own surfaces, and transformation imposed upon the consciousness and visual capacity of its inhabitants. That gesture produces two imageries: the virulent blur and babel of the city's surfaces, and the imageries transplanted into the heads of the city's inhabitants. The two resulting arenas of imagery demand a careful manipulation by any filmmaker of the city, since those imageries exist and produce their visual impact in resistantly autonomous but interdependent zones. It is a cross-contamination of the city and the viewer, designed to send a film reeling away into the endless proliferations of contradiction. The contradiction of an imagery of the human figure and the city, to aspire to authenticity, must be consciously incited, induced and reassembled as an exploration. The European city exists to deny and contradict itself; as a result, it contradicts its own progeny of imagery too. The abrasive momentum and vivid coloration fired off from the process of contradiction illuminate and transmit that imagery to the individual viewer of the city. The city is a site of endurance and survival: the invocative power of language holds itself in protective tension against the enveloping imageries of the city, constructing a barrier of text between the identity of the city's vocal inhabitant and the invasive visual impulse of the city. In Phil Jutzi's 1931 film of Döblin's *Berlin Alexanderplatz*, Heinrich George as Franz Biberkopf stands at the intersection of the city *incorporating* a declarative flood of text, expelling a vocabulary so dense as to be corporeal: glossolaliac particles and nodes of language aimed effusively at the hostile structure of the city. Biberkopf vocalizes existence in the city by means of its absences (the massing of the matter of language compensates him for the loss of his amputated arm, for the murder of his companion Mieze in the forests outside Berlin). Around his expectorated wall of text, the film traces the gestural detail of the metropolitan saturation of move-ment – amassed gestures of workers, of children, in juxta-position with the gestures of machinery, of vehicles. The imagery of the city intimates, in the potential escalation of confrontation between image and text, between human figure and city, that it is forever subject to its own obliteration (every external surface filmed in *Berlin Alexanderplatz* would disappear in the wartime bombing and postwar reinvention of the space, so that the present Alexanderplatz now has an absolutely different surface and text, though the filmed gestural detail of its visual chaos remains strongly recogniz-able and haunting). To create a permanently transforming cinema of the contemporary European city would demand a prescient and seismographic grip of the processes of transfor-mation – the accumulations, multiplications and dispersals of imagery on the surface of the city, the sudden oscillations between sensation and nullification in the identities of the cities' inhabitants. It would require, too, a vocabulary of imagery flexible enough to hold and project the immense contradiction of the European city. It is a contradiction which the future of Berlin and every European city holds behind its back, as a weapon, as a joke, as an instrument of its own obliteration. The force of contradiction in the city can only be imagined or, better still, creatively hallucinated into exist-ence, by the filmmaker who imprints an imagery upon the ferociously fragile existence of the future European city.

39

The corruption of the European cities is a tidal flood with no regulation, no pattern of submerging and withdrawing. The corruption of socialism in eastern Europe has been suc-ceeded by a pervasive corruption of the detail of life in the cities. The lucidity of the daily trajectory has been replaced by strategies of uncertain duration, supplemented by a dull and decreasing exhilaration of purposelessness. The human movements and gestures of corruption in the cities are those of an affrontment, person to person, repeated in a rhythm of abrasure which shreds the screen between human conscio-usness and the city, between identity and a chaotic, prolifer-ating intrusion. Corruption is ferally amalgamated from independence and mendacity: the corrupted inhabitants of the European city seek to induce a vivid presence and movement for themselves against the surface of the city (a comet trail accumulating a detritus of goods, cash, visual attributes). The collisions between those manoeuvres, over crack or over extortion or over raw territory, add noise to the already cacophonic aura of the peripheral districts of the city. The appearance of corruption never settles: it retracts momentarily into invisibility, then randomly blares and glares. The visual tracery of corruption embeds itself tenaciously into the facade of the city, as signals oscillating between threats and advertisements (advertising the denu-dation of existence). But however strongly it may implant its apparition as an element of the city's reality, corruption is ephemeral in its welding with the matter of the city, which is omnisciently indifferent and pivots on a central act of abjection. Corruption cannot acidically layer itself into the city as history, since the sources of its influx are intangible, interchangeable, and periodically combust without trace.

The action of corruption upon the city is instantly excessive and grotesque; it consumes the visual arena of the city in a bogus transaction (of void currencies of imagery) that cannot sustain itself and disintegrates bluntly, ineptly. Corruption is unsustainable; it will be replaced by a new configuration, which bursts bloodily out from within itself, or else arrives as a sudden violent invasion from another, exhausted zone of corruption. The transformation and sudden mutation of corruption in the streets of the European cities is a seduction whose visual sensation is one of disorientation, of surrender to assimilation. The framework of corruption, from the dimension of governmental institutions to the dimension of the slightest detail of metropolitan life, makes the inhabitants of the city inhabit a waste ground of their consciousness: they are exiled to a bizarre zone of tense numerical exchanges, where identity is abstracted and pulverized.

40

The language of the European cities is held at the interstice between silence and an ultimately voluble and rhythmic rush of words. Vast sections of the European city's population will not speak to equally vast elements, in a network of indifferences, hostilities, oversights: the perceptions of existence and identity that articulate the city are irretrievably disparate, while language in its exterior manifestation is a homogenized instrument of openness or denial. The language of the city explodes from silence. That silence may have originated in self-suppression – in the power of the refusal to communicate, the power not to speak – or in the collision of randomly opposed consciousness, from which unintelligibility issues. The language of the cities is a great contaminated mixing, which simultaneously generates impact and fissuration. To become attached to the furnace of imagery which the city drives, language passes in intimacy through intricate trajectories of exploration and interrogation, through unspeakable traversals of deadends and ellipses. The extreme experience of the city is the crossing of a *border* which sets language into upheaval, exposing and testing language. Language is alternately drained and saturated by its own riotous clashes with the vital matter of the city. The trajectory of language through the city is shadowed and countered by its erosion – even the most uniquely intense, vertiginous projection of language (a scream in the street, a whisper of ecstasy) will collapse in its act of realization, and lapse into silence. On the trains which cross the densely marked, effusively visual city of eastern Berlin, I listen to the conversations between tightly grouped inhabitants of the city (even five years after the dismantling of the Stasi, the instinct of the city's inhabitants is to conspire quietly, to judge the city secretively). The conversation collects a mass of exclamations which glances against the surface of the city – a complaint against its detail reinforced by exasperation at its totality. When exasperation is compacted and intensified by words into a state of silence, then that silence is a monopoly: the inhabitant of the city dominates the city by the unique refusal of its language. The silence is a conglomeration of anger, irony and the experience of the city. The inhabitant stares out, and absorbs the city. Then language starts again, cut with the visual impetus of the city and its transforming screens of imagery. The language of the city counters that imagery, is permeated by it, expectorates it, and exists through it.

41

The European city propagates oblivion: the streets of the city
are struck into astonishment by their transformation, and
forget themselves. The contours of the European city
become a terrain of forgetfulness, where every lucid
memory and sustained image of history is precariously
underpinned, liable at any instant to be overturned from
clarity to virtuality. The memory of the European city is
unbearable: its inhabitants are acutely exposed to the untied
sutures of memory in the surface of the city, and to protect
and screen themselves they misremember, view the sutures
of the city at a tangent, skim the city, pick out the inconsequential detail beside the glaring mark of calamity. The
misreading of the city as an act of oblivion becomes habitual,
an essential element of daily life in the city; without a partial,
intentional blindness, the memory of the city would grind
its inhabitants into its surface pitilessly, impose itself on
their visual perception with relentless excoriation. The
inhabitants traverse the city *in absentia*, averting their eyes
from its respiring obscenity. The will for metropolitan
survival generates an intricate performance of catalepsy; the
inhabitants of the city do not fear being buried alive (as did
Brecht, who instructed that a stiletto pierce his heart before
his burial) – they desire, instead, that the constant revivifi-
cation of the city's surface be entombed, since the virulent
gestures and projections of its memory accumulate into a
suffocation of inhabitation. On television, the oblivion of the
city is lamented, condemned. Reports focus on the traces of
memory which have undergone an ellipsis of their partici-
pation in the linear, temporal consciousness of the city; the
intensity of the atrocity in those memories, if *remembered*,
provokes a necessary disruption, an upheaval, in the vec-

tors of the city's consciousness. The transition of memory into television imagery gives it endurance (in the momentary and volatile atmosphere of televisual time and space) but makes it endurable: the desire for oblivion is sated in the flux of imagery around memory's evocation. Memories are selected according to their criteria as prime-time material for resuscitation into history. The imperative is to make memory new, make atrocity new, but also to control its visual and sensational threshold. The filtering of memory from its presence on the surface of the city into its representation on television or on film is a process which removes both its raw charge and its banality: the inexhaustible screen of memory is channelled and projected as the unique memory of visual ingestion. The oblivious spectator of the city surveys and selects the configuration of memory which will provide the sensation of inhabiting the city and its historical layers, and also gauges the emanation which that memory will transmit. It is the power and intention of vision which constructs and creates the extraordinary in the European city.

The cities of Europe cannot exist alone. The lines, motor-
ways, channels between the cities are the entangled ephemera that destroy the autonomy of each city. Europe is the site
at which heterogeneous imageries and languages collide
and then bind together to produce an identity which the city
exists to exude. The space outside the city is always an ugly
scene, the warning signs for which flash in the catastrophic
periphery, where amalgams of violent concrete and violent
gang warfare intimate the tension of a trajectory bordering
on the void. Leaving the city, the elaborately accumulated
hallucination of the city cruelly evanesces (though stub-
bornly survives, at vision's edge, gesturing to the inhabitant
possessed by nostalgia, visible at a cost, through a contorted
ocular manoeuvre). The exit from the city is a release in
terms of exhilaration, and a self-exemption from the
network of visual responsibility exacted by the city from its
inhabitant (who compulsively contributes a permanent act
of vision to the matter of the city, to ascertain and to realize
its existence). The inhabitant of the city is a visually addicted
creature, and the city serves to double that addiction. For
the inhabitant of the city in transit, the loss of that compulsively addicting perception is a wretched denudation: the city
is indispensable, irreplicable, in the interzone before the
subsequent city is reached. The dispossessed inhabitant
searches for the gravitational axis to the images and texts of
the new city, which dynamically shift and swarm but do not
touch or cohere. The instinct of the exile is to elaborate a
provisional vocabulary for the white noise and rush of
imagery, so that perception tentatively approaches the
momentarily inassimilable carapace of the new city, which is
itself simultaneously approaching and disassembling its

chaos in response to the escalation of vision which each new act of inhabitation in the new city consolidates. The primary experience of the endlessly heterogeneous European city enables a reconstitution of the new city as a surrogate of the abandoned city. But the process of establishing vision, establishing language, is incessantly intercut by the expulsive force of the city, which incessantly refuses and jettisons the invasive gesture of its new inhabitant's identity. Journeys between the European cities possess their own vocabulary of nomadic limbo and of imminent engulfment by the succession of cities. The traveller between the cities is absorbed by the process of oscillation and anticipation (the next city is the traveller's ultimate captivation); by determining the rhythm of those voids and saturations, the traveller creates an *instance of Europe* which is welded from the elements of its cities.

43

The populations of the European cities exist in a state of sustained self-absorption, watching the infrastructure of their identity shatter, the minutiae of their perception erode. The process of inhabiting the cities is a casting of consciousness into hypnotized disarray: the city hooks the eye into a captivated act of vision, but the imagery transmitted into the eye proliferates effusively, will not cohere, and throws the inhabitant's perception into brittle isolation. When the inhabitant of the European city contemplates identity, it is inescapably in juxtaposition with the determining city. The city's population groups and amasses in order to sustain identity against its visual subjugation. The group of inhabitants gestures and gazes in reaction against the temporal slippage, the territorial dispossession, the transfusion of a contaminated identity, which the city's imagery precipitates. The group signals that it possessed identity and a stable life in the city, a moment ago, and that the sudden corrosion which has overtaken that identity can be reversed, rectified, with imminent effect. The prolongation of the delay before identity can be seized is inexplicable, insufferable; and the group of inhabitants fractures into isolation once again. The constant impulse towards amalgamation in the city's population animates the city's surface, which becomes strewn with the mutating configurations of human groupings, adhered anti-organically into units of consumption, corruption, production. The group constructs order within itself in the expectation that it will generate a power of cogency, a counter-imagery to the influx of the city. The more tightly the group is sealed, the more open it is to a random perforation from the city, which will crack through any fabricated environment or imagery. The group is at its most abrasive when it exposes itself provocatively to the matter of the city, by its inhabitation of the marginal streets and wretched interstices of the city. Each sliding site of the city is the precarious colony of the grouped homeless, the neo-nazis, the alcoholics, the punks (exhausted by the endless repetition of their signals). When the group spills into the street, it cancels and abandons its circular movement of absorption. It instigates a trajectory which diverges from the intention of the group: the city is then subjected to the caprice of violent human movement along its tarmac arteries. Such a gesture fluctuates between negation and electrification in its impact on the city: it may extinguish itself in a raw, damaging collision with the surface of the city and its imagery. Or it may engender a burning haemorrhage of transformation that courses uncontrollably through the city, and projects the active dimension of a human grouping *upon* the city. Then new imageries of the city are created.

44

Fragments of the European city: each amalgam of image and text that transmits the city is an autonomous fragment of the intricately assembled, relentlessly disassembling metropolitan screen. The European city is transformed at the level of its fragments, which are inassimilable to a homogeneous, enduring formation. The infinite permutation of disintegration and reconstitution in the city's fragments of imageries, fragments of languages, is the dominant dynamic force in the projection of the city to its spectators. The city oscillates between impact and chaos in order to articulate itself; its central axis lies in contradiction. The issue of that contradiction opens the city to chance, so that cities with parallel processes of visual transformation may alternately be inhabited by incessant outbreaks of violence, or by an utter stasis and banality. The fragment of the city does not mirror the entirety of the city, since the city does not possess an encompassing entirety; the city is bound in interactive resistance with a random conglomeration of other fragments which constitute the vividly fluctuating arena of the visual city. The tension of that arena is intensified by the seismically unstable layers of the city's history, which (however well camouflaged or subject to oblivion they may be) will resurge at will into the present of the city. The consciousness of the city is correspondingly fragmentary. The institutional will to direct the imagery of the city, control its channels, give it internal priorities, cannot be synchronized across the city; that will itself is subject to the bizarre obsessions which are integral to institutional bodies, so that the imprinting of institution upon the city's surface is saturated at one point with ambitious configurations (architectural, monumental) of surreal and heated over-orchestration, and entirely absent at another point. The most sustained and lurid saturation of imagery emerged from the institutions of the DDR. The collapse of that imagery – with the instantaneous loss of consciousness suffered by its institutions – produced a spectacular fragmentation of vision in the DDR's cities which, in an inverse process of parallel instantaneity, was reabsorbed and tenuously modulated by the influx of imagery (equally alien, more uniformly riven) from western Germany. The setting of institutional parameters for con-sciousness in the city's imagery – censorship and elision of cinema, advertising, television imagery – produces an in-tricate but arbitrary network of prohibition and victimization (added to the already precarious dynamics of represen-tation). Prohibition of consciousness amasses where it is most systematically, furiously opposed, and otherwise drains and disperses through consciousness. The spectator of the European city engages in a constant gestural manipu-lation of the fragments transmitted to consciousness; the movement generated by that dealing with the matter of the city, visually rejecting and transacting, physically traversing and skimming, creates a dense rhythm of fragmentation. The language of every fragment must be collated with its imagery, with its noise – the components stripped down, with utter brevity, as raw material for identity.

45

Every memory visualized by the European city – in its museums, its monuments – is the result of the processes of self-reflection and self-filtration used by the city to determine its identity. Any identity which the city may project is mediated between the screens and voids of the past and the unsluiced velocity of the present. The contemporary cities of Europe are acutely overexposed: in the present city, everything can be seen, glaringly; nothing can be hidden. The past of the city is intimately compromised, the present integrally and compulsively complicit: the marks of the past bear indelible witness to the attempts to obliterate their presence in the city. The museums of the city exhibit a compulsion to enact and show the damage of the raw past. The city is bound by the ligatures of its voluble, visual, inscribed history. The selection of material for the city's 'museums of identity' necessarily involves an excision of particular elements from its history, counterposed by the compacting and telescoping of identity around other elements – manoeuvred from isolated interstices of history to form superficially organic configurations. The amputation and transplantation of the material and imagery of history into the transmissible form of vital memory is the most sensitive process in the gathering of identity for the city. The version of the city which is created supplants previous identities, the traces of which suffer a sudden, random diminution of their visual presence, so that determined elements of the city's history become peripheral, located far beyond the habitual visual trajectories of the city's inhabitants. Each 'museum of identity' must project itself as immediate and definitive in its assembling of the facts of memory; it forecloses the future. The European cities are peripherally inhabited by a multiplicity of lost museums – of neglected, effaced identities, which oppose or contradict the identity which effectively controls and illuminates the city's history. The resuscitation and reconstruction of a discarded history demands a sustained act of excavation and restitution of memory, such as that involved in the opening of the Wannsee Museum of the Holocaust in Berlin, located in the actual villa at which Heydrich formulated the detailed plan for the Final Solution in 1942. The villa was used for decades as a lakeside recreation centre for children, its significance obscured, in the city where the leading neo-nazi Arnulf-Winfried Priem uses a machine-gun burst instead of an electronic beep on his answering machine. On the other side of Berlin, the transformation of the Stasi headquarters into a museum was almost instantaneous: the saturation of the city's identity by the Stasi necessitated an immediate mutation of sensation (oppression on the most extreme level of banality and fear) into memory as an act of liberation, entangled equally instantly with irony, nostalgia. The museums define and project their set of images against the city's monumentally enveloping flood of imagery and of vision, and within the tenacious survival of historical fact and upheaval into the present of the city's identity.

46

The European city swathes its inhabitants in a responsive medium of noise, which intimates the upheavals and rhythms of the city to its listener, just as it transmits the languages, the protests, the cries of the inhabitants into the matter of the city. Each moment in the city is possessed by a dense coagulation of noise fragments that are dynamically oscillating, thrown from the city to human perception, from human perception back to the city. The momentary node of the city's noise seizes a presence in the city by its multiple abrasure into the surfaces of the city and of consciousness; but from that original act of seizure, the noise of the city becomes instantly passive – to temporal extinguishment, and to its seepage into the surface and dimension of the city. The noise of the city is also subject to the infinite human ability to ignore noise, to discard noise, as extraneous. And the inhabitants of the city possess the capacity to reinvent and manipulate the components of noise – in their heads or in the form of music – into new assemblages that seize and counterpoint the sensation of dislocation that their identities encounter in intimate contact with the city. The dispersal of noise around the streets of the city presents creative raw material for musicians and performers who reassemble the debris of the streets as instruments, and reassemble the rejected imageries of the city's surface as the accompaniment to the transmutation of noise. But left to run wild – or subjected to an excess of discipline – noise will hum and pulse incessantly in the city. It is fluid, utterly palpable and extensible (the inverse of the volatile, fierce stuff of imagery, the intricately resistant material of text). Although the noise of the city is a void which is intrinsically open to the influx of an aggressive charge, its own movements, gestures, rhythms, vocabularies are unremittingly benign. In the nightclubs, derelict factories and warehouses of Berlin, the vocabularies of noise double the vocabularies of dance: an absolute repetition which exhilarates the heartbeat into its own, urgently beating repetition. On their daily round, the inhabitants of the city experience noise at sensorial interstices and peripheries (when the visual arena of the city intermittently breaks down, when the aural languages of the city accidentally blare); the trajectory which the inhabitants take through their city directs every shift in the level and sensation of noise. Perception respires a sheer minimum of noise in the city streets, taking in a necessary detail of noise for guidance, a controlled impact of noise for pleasure. Otherwise, noise is screened away and lapses. Without that screening, the volume of noise would escalate with linearity, from moment to moment, from exasperation to overload. It is when the inhabitants of the city are themselves static, in a state of tension (in a waiting room, on an underground train) that the static accumulation of noise rips spatially and intrudes into consciousness, as an unbearable invasion of the city. The inert consciousness concentrates itself to expel noise as an element of the city, magnifies each fracture of noise to outrageous proportions as a threatened inflammation of exposed consciousness. The inhabitant of the city hallucinates the obliteration of noise, desires silence; when movement starts over again, the desire for noise regenerates itself.

47

The sensation of culture in the contemporary European city
is a drained and splintered presence. If the cities possess any
culture at all now, its strength lies only in the utter inter-
changeability of its elements, which can be juxtaposed and
transformed to jar creatively against the transformation of
the city. While the inhabitants of the city habitually experience a central nervous paralysis in their rapport with
culture, they can be randomly attracted by its visual spill, its
amalgamations, its ricochets and its repetitions. Cultures
which compound hopelessness, which offer white noise,
generate hypnotized affection from the shattered city's
traumatized inhabitants. Since the surviving fragments of
culture lack structures or intentions, are wildly undetermined and mobile, they become voracious in their
encounter with the surfaces of the city: the city is subjugated
to the viral configurations of culture, which impetuously
construct and collapse in on themselves. In the decades after
the Second World War, the carapace of institutionally
imposed culture over the cities of both western and eastern
Germany made those indigestibly scarred cities soluble to
consciousness. Now, for the inhabitants of the contemporary eastern German city, the idea of culture still generates a
nostalgia of great depth, which is attached to sites rather
than imageries or languages. Even the pre-fabricated concrete cultural 'palaces' of the DDR still project grandiose
apparitions of themselves which radiate from their risible,
increasingly derelict sites. Any culture which survives in the
European city is now attached to the ecstasy and devastation
of the human figure. The imagery of the body in the city (in
video, film, photography, painting) creates an infinite gestural vocabulary of violent, intentional, sexual acts which

are transmitted from the matter of the image to the matter of the human figure inhabiting the city. The body as image is the ultimate axis of fragmentation: nothing can engender such an extreme oscillation between abstraction and viscerality, between nuanced intuition and raw tangibility. The fragment of the body always incorporates a fragment of the city. The European city is convulsed by a visual culture of the figure which is multiply open to permutations with other bodies, and with every imagery and medium. Urban culture can hold intensities of imagery, but cannot project them with an immediacy of sensation: its channels of representation are jammed by overuse and misuse, and perforated by the wounding history of the European city and its present voids (of racism, of oppression, of corruption). The city's culture subsists as an instrument of vital amalgamation, producing imageries into which the inhabitants of the city display or discard the extreme sensations of their lives.

48

In the cinemas of the European cities, the spectators
accumulate a momentum of vision, from the rhythm of the
film, from the dynamics of the figures' movements and the
dynamics of montage, which they then transmit to the
momentum of the city. The intersection between the ocular
experience of the film and the succeeding ocular experience of the city is vertiginous – momentarily and spatially.
The sound of the film is ultimately sutured, either through
the closing music or simply by the silence that comes with
the end of the image, but the internal dissonance of the
film is reactivated, opened out to the cacophony of the
city, when the spectator steps into the street. The act of
watching in the cinema does not generate a site of autonomy, since it is always intercut with the ineradicable
stratification of the imagery of the city into the spectator's
consciousness. Even in the space of the cinema, the film
spectators are compulsively aware of their position within
the world of the city, and that awareness resists and
overrides the world of the film; the powerful heterogeneity
of the city street's imagery is rarely exceeded by that of the
film. Absorption in the film is an alternation of perception
to that determined by an inhabitation of the city;
perception contracts or diffuses away from the visual regulation of the city. But absorption is launched from the
narratives of the city, from the habitual visual vocabularies
of the city, which permeate the trajectory of viewing and
its realization of film cities; however imaginary or surreal
the origins of the film city may be, its evocative impact is
created by the intricate entanglement which the act of
watching develops between the city on film and the city
which envelops the cinema. The adhesive proximity of the

external city's screen of imagery to the cinema's screen of imagery gives the act of viewing its original, exhilarated edge of pre-eminence over the city (a cancellation which rapidly collapses into suspension of the city, as the film progresses linearly, diminishing temporally while its internal dynamics, its rhythms of sound and image, escalate). Across the European cities, cinemas vividly punctuate the endless city streets; they withdraw into dereliction, transform and proliferate as multiplexes. The cinemas are atmospherically inhabited by the former use of their buildings: cinemas in Berlin that had their origin in a slaughterhouse, a luxurious hotel ballroom, a Stasi entertainment palace. In the cinemas of the Albanian cities, the apparition of the film image is miraculous; the ellipsis which film time provokes within the duration of the unbearable city is persistently extended, so that each prolonged reel change becomes the occasion for a sustained blare of voices and anticipation. The European city is an ineptly edited arrangement, crazily synchronized, that relentlessly projects its imageries into a multiplicity of channels, spatially and temporally somersaulting, infinitely extensible. The cinemas fall prey to the static uniqueness of their space, under the pressure of that relentlessness, and conglomerate luxuriously into the material of the city (into shopping centres, into industrial estates), eroding the vital membrane between the identity of the film spectator and the identity of the city's inhabitant.

49

Every night, the television stations of the European cities condense and project the arena of imageries relating to language, history, culture, violence, society, sexuality in the city. Across Europe, the components of that projection are endlessly variable, indissolubly disparate: welded into cultural and historical sources that are exposed to up-heavals of rearrangement, exaggeration, obscuration. The capacity of the television station technically to amass the sources at its disposal is vital to its translation of informa-tion into representation – without an array of images to discard, the television station cannot display its intention to generate an identity between the city and the television spectator (the poverty of images is the ultimate stigma for the television station). But confronted with a bank of imagery which is infinitely extensible (in every dimension: spatially, through all the European cities; temporally, through every moment of the visually rendered historical past; and telescopically, through every last detail and pano-rama of metropolitan inhabitation), the television station must create an exclamatory texture for the representation of its news transmission. Intricate narratives of events in the city are amalgamated into blunt coherence, minute details of the city are inflated and diffused into evocation: the compilation of the news events fluidly traverses borders and languages as it compacts idioms and styles. The status of a television station of a European metropolis is in tension with its status as a national channel, as a cross-European channel: the station collects its content nationally, inter-nationally, and directs its trajectory at close range (so that the impact of the transmission's imagery is experienced in proportion to the viewer's incorporation in, or exclusion from, metropolitan identity). The receptive inhabitant attuned to the visual and textual vocabularies and emphases of a particular city extrapolates national and European identity – with fluctuating degrees of empathy and opposition – from the multiple configuration presented by the television station of one metropolitan identity. The trajectory from the metropolis to nation to Europe has its source in the imagery of city streets and buildings as the site of exchanges, decisions, acts of violence and reconciliation; the perception of the television viewer moves out from individual experience in the city to alien exteriority, and returns to the city with a visual residue which is the articulation of Europe as a dual material: Europe is enticing and threatening, is immanent and distant, is present and void. Europe is an identity that exists through images, through language: it is utterly subject to its creation at the point of meshing between the visual and the textual. The television stations of Europe are vital to the generation of that site, which may be an axis for interactive identity between the cities, or an axis of inflammation (any detail of xenophobia cultivates and magnifies itself in the medium of television, with its vast visual sway and vastly susceptible audience); cross-European television channels work to dis-integrate the insularity of a domination of imagery by the city, to open out and intensify the transaction of vision between European television and its spectator.

50

In the final years of the twentieth century, all the cities of Europe are seen through the great hallucination of the city of Berlin. Whatever can now be seen of the future of Europe has its site of origin in the contemporary moment of Berlin. However incoherent the present moment in Berlin may be – and the human eye is perpetually blurred and blinded by the virulent velocity of contemporary Berlin – that city remains the crucial location at which the past history of Europe impacts into its own future. The future of Berlin is a roughly painted black cross already inscribed over the pure white expanse of the future of Europe: it can be viewed as a negative cancellation, or it can be viewed as a sign of creation that Europe must confront. The embedding of history, violence, obsession into the *visual present* is realized in its most vivid and intensely tangible form in the ongoing transformation of Berlin. The multiple trajectories of imagery which move at the speed of light through the European cities are suffused by, and issue from, that transformation. Berlin is a city of the 'desire to obliterate' – a desire that haunts Europe, that attracts, terrifies, animates Europe. The incubation of any transformation in Europe, however monstrous or revelatory, is heated in an atrocious narcotic rush by the imagery of Berlin. Berlin is the city which has irreparably wounded the twentieth century, and which takes ecstasy from the sensation of that wound – a wound which will bleed into the future. In its immense, chaotic sprawl, Berlin denies the claim that it possesses a 'myth'. Berlin has no myth, no legend; equally, there is no myth of Europe, simply an accumulation of fragments of exhilaration, stimulation, rapture: fragments of buildings, of faces, of images. In Berlin, it becomes clear that what is most gruelling in the experience of Europe is only minutely screened from what is most superficial and trivial; the assimilation of the superficial detail emanating from Berlin involves a parallel, necessary swallowing of a harsh, toxic content which is indigestible – the screen of vision in Berlin is uniquely insubstantial. The everyday traversal of Berlin is an intricate manoeuvre through a gaping terrain of ash, adrenalin and voids. To reach the far side of that terrain is to arrive in the heart of the future of Europe. The contemporary landscape of Berlin is more than haunting; it is *lacerating*. The transformations of the city – the immense building work in the eastern parts of the city, the sudden apparition of endless graffiti surfaces – only affirm that laceration. From the raw gap in the matter of Europe, Berlin will be propelled into its future as a vertiginously destabilizing force for the identity of the European city. Berlin is the trigger of Europe, always convulsed at the moment before the act of ignition. Europe's limits and parameters are in a constant state of collapse, and the repercussions and jolts of that process collect in Berlin and provide it with its disturbed polyphony of voices: the level of vocal noise in the city is relentless, pitched between anxiety and fantasy (every life in Berlin, however transient or temporary, is a fantasy life in imminent danger of exposure) – and rendered in a mass of languages, dialects, expectorations. Every moment experienced in the city grates identity further and further away from itself, from its source, and the interstice is occupied by the vocal interrogation of a sensation of loss (a vocal texture of anger, exile, nostalgia, astonished bewilderment). Berlin acts to create an exact visual seismography of its own violent identity: the layers of image and noise form a transparent medium over the contemporary city through which the inhabitant looks down into the wreckage of the city's

history. Berlin's exhibition of itself is compulsive and capti-
vating. The lucidity of the city, in its gesture of upheaval, is
an instrument of vision that projects out across all the cities
of Europe. Berlin is the vital element in the configuration of
the contemporary and future European city. It is the city
which initiates an exploration of the process of seeing, the
damage to seeing, the multiplicity of seeing, since Berlin
simultaneously manifests its precipitation of scarred space
and the cancellation of that space. The survival of the image
and the survival of the act of vision in the European city rest
upon the interactive resistance between that city and its
defiant inhabitant. Nothing exists of the city but dupli-
cation, repetition and prolongation, except for what is put
there by the eye of the spectator, intercepted and visually
substantiated. And with the falling of the eye upon the city
comes the massive movement, gesture, flux of physical
incorporation of the city, that gives to the city its psychosis
of imagery and language, the amalgam of banality and
explosivity, its wildness, fragmentation, transformation.